Keeping in

Managing Your Mental Health

To Nicola,

You are stronger than you realise.

Keep Fighting!

LB

Laura Bartlam

First Published in 2024 by Laura Bartlam
with Russell-Alexander Publishing Ltd

Edited by Russell-Alexander Publishing Ltd

Cover Design by Catherine Parry of Paper Chameleons

Photography by Amy Kelly

ISBN: 978-1-66640-740-2

Contents

Dedications

This book is dedicated to the people who have held me up, who have stayed by my side no matter what and who have walked every step of my recovery journey with me. You are my people, my tribe and my reason for fighting to keep my bipolar disorder stable.

To Steve, my incredible husband, and to a love that has stood the test of time, especially the vow of "in sickness and in health"; you never gave up on me, no matter how mentally unwell I was. When I had lost all sense of myself, you gently guided me and helped me reclaim my identity. Your love and support is unfaltering.

To my son Matthew; it's not easy having a mum who isn't always totally present. You're my buddy and being off work for long periods of time gave me the opportunity to spend more time with you and to be your personal chauffeur which is when we had our best chats. You've also had your own health issues and I'm incredibly proud of your resilience and strength.

To my Mum and stepdad, Allen. Mum, you are my rock and I am yours. Your unconditional love and belief that I could overcome anything life threw my way spurred me on. I'm incredibly blessed to have inherited your strength, compassion, integrity and wisdom.

To my brother, Stewart, my sister-in-law, Suz and nephew, Coby. I am thankful to have a brother who is also one of my best friends; who had my back during my darkest days and who was my advocate when I couldn't do it myself. I'm thankful for our long chats on the phone putting the world to rights and for family days together, fun and laughter.

My family have loved and cared for me throughout this extraordinary journey and have kept me motivated when times were really tough.

To Fudge, who ensured I was never alone; who made me go for walks outside and who introduced me to an incredible group of new friends who provide endless support and with whom I can be completely myself

Last but not least, to the latest addition to our family, Foggy, who has brought me joy and happiness. I can’t believe you are the same little girl who came to us four years ago dishevelled and terrified of the world; you are beautiful and brave. You remind me of my journey from darkness into light and love, my precious girl.

Foreword

Beginning.

(Everyone starts somewhere).

'I often refer to peer support as magical'....

As I read through the sections of this book that Laura has sent to me so that I can write this foreword, this line stands out because I agree so strongly. Peer support is magical; through a combination of safe space, time, respect, equality, equity, listening ears, opportunity to speak and genuine heartfelt care for the wellbeing of all involved, it transforms and brings out the magic in people. I have witnessed firsthand, many times, the return of the spark of life that so often can be lost in the midst of illness and a huge life change.

Laura, who is writing this book, and who has been a person looking for support to heal and grow, then peer support participant, volunteer, staff member, and role model for many, is an absolutely magical person. She is a person with stories to share, powerful stories of survival, learning and recovery, some of which she captures in these wonderful pages.

She is someone who has the ability to face the difficult stuff with openness and honesty, to do the work to learn, to put that learning into practice, resulting in growth and evolution, and then to, from the heart, use that knowledge for the good of others. The result? Her ongoing work, in support of those who are healing and growing, within peer support, her own business, and this writing.

I could cry at the beauty of this book existing. I remember meeting Laura for the first time when she bravely walked through the doors at Leeds Mind seeking support. I had made it, after my own experience of walking the recovery path, I too had been a person looking for support to heal and grow, then a peer support participant, a volunteer, and I had become a staff member, and role model. I connected straight away with the expression on her face. I could see it then...amongst the uncertainty, anxiety, and also excitement, of new things...I could see her grim determination. The determination of someone who has 'been there'. This stuff was not going to beat her, she came to soak all of the learning in, to equip herself with all she would need to be able to go ahead, repair, and grow strongly. I became a companion, and facilitator, walking next to her, as others had walked alongside me as I found my way.

Laura writes about her experiences in peer support, 'how fantastic for me to see someone with the same diagnosis in this role and sharing how they have learned techniques to manage their condition', and goes on to say, 'I think what amazed me most was that someone could see that potential in me, something I thought was gone forever'. At that time there was a big team of us, every person had made their way up from square one to being king of their own castle, but there were no egos flying around, only the desire to help others make the climb successfully.

Now Laura is paying it forwards too. This is a book, designed to be written peer support, which means that information about tools and techniques is shared, this is then 'coloured in' by how those things have worked or not worked for Laura herself, followed by an invitation to choose what is right for you, and to adapt it all for yourself as an individual, and then there are links included to places that you can go to for further information. 'The biggest thing here, in my opinion, is choice', Laura says, and I agree, choice has also been key for me and my own recovery.

Over the years, Laura, and I, have joked that we are very similar, many times, and I identify with so much of what she writes about, not just because I know her but because it makes sense. I hope you will find this too in the elements of physical, mental, emotional health included - ones that Laura helps come alive, and makes real, through the sharing of her personal experiences.

Laura writes in a very relatable, very real, very honest, very open way - you can hear that she goes through this stuff too, right now, in the present moment. She shares herself and her voice in this book, and you can get to know her, through the things she has learnt to do – the very useful tools and techniques that she describes in detail, and also through the stories of who she is and how she individualises those tools and techniques in relation to herself as a human 'being. 'Keeping in balance' is a very appropriate title for this book, as Laura writes about the balance between 'doing' and 'being'; what she does and who she is, skills she has and the experiences of using them to support herself, the analysis and head-based reflection of those experiences, and the body-based feelings that were there too.

I particularly enjoyed the way Laura has been able to capture, in black and white text, the running, racing, conversation of anxiety-related thoughts, that can often seem so abstract, hidden, and hard to explain, here, they are written in a way that made me go 'yeah, I recognise that, it happens to me too'. There is comfort in hearing that others go through these things as well.

The thing about peer support and recovery is that it becomes a lifestyle and a mindset, not just something you do and so this stuff that Laura is writing about is the very real way that she lives her life, it is woven through her like the words in a stick of rock, and so it can be trusted to be the core of all of this, it is in everything she does, every decision she makes, every interaction she has. She lives the recovery life; she has levelled up.

Recovery, from my experience, is a process of observing the self, and noticing the patterns that are happening within ourselves and then working on those, not a process of following what other people think we should be doing. Laura has the experience of this happening for herself in real life and intends this book to perhaps be the spark for you, the reader, to find the way towards growth and transition for yourself.

So, as you read from page to page, and walk, step by step, with Laura, from the Poisonous Parrot and Wise Owl, to the Stress Bucket, to the Wellbeing Flower, through the shared experiences of train journeys, cord cutting experiences, lightbulb moments and learning in relationships, and witness the honest reflections on medication, caffeine, sleep, alcohol and much, much more, I wish you safety, the ability to face things head on, permission to shape your own tools, to use your own voice and find your recovery language, to ask for support when you need it, to find your tribe, and to mess up and be able to learn as much from those experiences as you can from the ones that go well.

"You are the driving force in your recovery."

Wisdom, written by the person I, Sue Bird, am privileged to call my friend, and once colleague, Laura Bartlam.

Sue Bird

From the Author

Life sometimes throws you a curveball; usually, it's totally unexpected, happens in a split second and sends you flying off on a tangent that you never expected. Well, that's exactly what happened to me except my curveball came in the form of a 52-seater coach that crashed into my car. A night out to watch my brother's band ended with a lift to the train station in the back of a police car and not getting to the venue or seeing the band perform.

At that point in my life, I was working full-time as a Special Needs teacher, completing a 15-month leadership course with a view to applying for Assistant Head Teacher positions and studying for a Postgraduate Diploma in Multisensory Impairment. In hindsight, this was far too much for me to do at once and, when we had the accident, if I wasn't there already, I was well on my way to burnout. I'm convinced that this contributed to the severity of the mental health issues that followed and now I'm very aware of how much I'm trying to cram into my life.

What I choose to do now follows careful consideration and, usually, conversations with my family and friends to ensure that I don't reach that point again. Quite often, I just have to say "no". If, like me, you are a "yes" person then finding ways to gain thinking time before responding can be invaluable. Here are a few "thinking time" responses for your toolbox:

"That sounds great but I need to check my calendar. I'll get back to you."

~

"I'm not sure. I'll let you know."

~

"Thanks for the invitation but I already have/think I have something on."

You don't have to say "no" but equally you don't have to say "yes" immediately. This was difficult for me at first but has become easier over time.

Back to the aftermath of the accident. At first, I was absolutely fine; I was calm and collected. I had whiplash but I knew that we were incredibly lucky as the outcome of the crash could have been much, much worse. I went straight back to work and generally got on with my life. I don't know exactly when I started to unravel but slowly and surely I did, as the changes in my mental health gained momentum and finally became like a runaway freight train! Then, after seeking expert medical advice, a diagnosis of Post-Traumatic Stress Disorder (PTSD) was confirmed and my treatment began. However, something else was happening; I didn't understand what it was and I couldn't verbalise it or find the right words to explain it. Eventually, I became so unwell that I was hospitalised and diagnosed with Bipolar Disorder.

In truth, it came as a relief to have a diagnosis and I began to learn about the condition and explore ways to find a balance for my moods.

For the past nine years, my mood has been stable and I've learned a wide range of strategies – some that help me and some that don't. Numerous lifestyle changes have been made, new routines have been formed and old habits thrown away. That's precisely what this book is about - the things I've found that enable me to live a fulfilling life whilst living with a well-controlled, but incurable, mental illness. Don't get me wrong; what works for me won't work for everyone and I'm constantly, and will have to continue, doing a variety of things to maintain and regulate my mood. I also continue to explore new ideas and learn new strategies.

You don't need to read this book from cover to cover as some of the conditions and treatments won't relate to your condition. Instead, flick through and select the parts that relate and appeal to you. Highlight the elements that really resonate with you and scribble in the margins as you would with any reference book. You will also find affirmations (short, positive statements that can be used to boost your well-being) and activities to try. In the "Just As It Is" sections you will find throughout the book, I've written about what is happening in my life, the effects on my mental health and what I've chosen to do to help redress the balance when times become tricky.

You don't need to have a diagnosis of Bipolar Disorder to find this book useful as there is a vast range of symptoms that apply to multiple mental health conditions. We all suffer from varying degrees of stress in our daily lives and anything that can help relax or ground us is excellent for our mental well-being. Most importantly, we all have mental health and it is important to look after it. My hope is that my book goes some way to helping you explore and manage your own mental health.

Laura Bartlam

About Mental Health Disorders

Post Traumatic Stress Disorder – PTSD

This condition was originally recognised in World War One veterans and was referred to as "shell shock". The term may have been used earlier than 1915 but the first written reference was in February 1915 in both The Times newspaper and The Lancet medical journal. Although the condition was first attributed to the effects of war, it is now recognised that it can develop in anyone following exposure to a traumatic event. It is, therefore, evident that people have suffered from PTSD since early civilisation when they faced significant life challenges due to disease, injury and predators. It wasn't until 1980 that the term Post-Traumatic Stress Disorder was used to encompass the symptoms being experienced by all people after traumatic events.

The causes of PTSD are varied. What one person finds traumatic, causing them considerable mental distress, may not have the same effect on someone else who is experiencing that same trauma. The following list of causes of PTSD is far from exhaustive:

- Car accident;
- Rape or sexual assault;
- Abuse, harassment or bullying (this includes racism, sexism, homophobia, biphobia, transphobia, etc.);
- Diagnosis of a life-threatening condition;
- Sectioning under the Mental Health Act;
- Violence (military combat, terrorist attack, domestic violence or violent assault);

- Kidnap;
- Witness to a traumatic event ("secondary trauma");
- Employment, for example, emergency services, where dealing with distressing events is part of the job;
- Natural disasters: flooding, earthquake, hurricane, etc;
- Traumatic childbirth either as the mother, her partner or the baby.

There are three kinds of PTSD

- ***Delayed onset PTSD***

  Having feelings of confusion and upsetting thoughts often occur if a person has experienced a traumatic event. For most people, these symptoms improve over a period of a few weeks. However, if the symptoms continue beyond four weeks, they should see their GP. For some people, the symptoms aren't felt immediately and it may be months or even years later when symptoms occur. This is known as "Delayed Onset PTSD."
- ***Complex PTSD***

  This term is used to describe PTSD where the person experienced trauma when they were very young; where the trauma lasted for a long time; where multiple traumas were experienced; or where someone they knew harmed them. It is referred to as CPTSD and there are often additional symptoms experienced with this condition.
- ***Birth Trauma***

  This term describes PTSD which develops following a traumatic experience during childbirth.

PTSD symptoms

The most common symptom of PTSD is the re-experiencing of the traumatic event. This may be experienced mentally in the form of flashbacks, nightmares, distressing images and/or sensations. Alternatively, it may be experienced physically in the form of pain, sweating, nausea and/or trembling. Trying to avoid the reminders of the traumatic event may cause the person to block out what occurred and to find distractions such as working too hard, filling their time with hobbies and avoiding anything that may stir up memories of the traumatic event. Self-harm may occur; self-harm is an intentional act of self-injury which is an expression of emotional distress and can include the misuse of drugs and/or alcohol. PTSD sufferers may also experience elevated levels of anxiety and feeling on edge. This is referred to as "Hyperarousal" and can lead to insomnia, anger, irritability and/or the inability to concentrate.

Treatment for PTSD

As with all mental illnesses, the symptoms and treatments may overlap. For PTSD, the main treatments are talking therapies and medication. Monitoring your own symptoms over time, to evaluate whether they are improving or worsening, can also help you to identify triggers that cause your anxiety and flashbacks.

The main talking therapies that PTSD sufferers access are Cognitive Behaviour Therapy ("CBT") and Dialectal Behaviour Therapy ("DBT"). CBT teaches practical coping skills for dealing with a variety of situations. It focuses on the impact of your thoughts, beliefs and attitudes on your feelings and actions. DBT is based on the same principles as CBT but has been specially adapted for those who experience very intense emotions. It enables people to understand and accept difficult emotions whilst learning skills to manage them.

Eye Movement Desensitisation and Reprocessing ("EMDR") is a highly effective treatment which was developed to help people process traumatic memories and see things from a different perspective which relieves their symptoms. Medication may also be prescribed with the antidepressants Paroxetine and Sertraline being the recommended medications in the UK.

My personal experience of PTSD

PTSD commonly occurs in people with mood disorders including Bipolar Disorder. In research studies, it has been found that people with Bipolar Disorder are ten times more likely to have a PTSD diagnosis than the general public. This fascinates me greatly; for me, it's a bit like the chicken and egg scenario - which came first?

On reflection, I can identify episodes of hypomania (a state of elevated mood, characterised by increased energy, exhilaration and irritability, associated with bipolar disorder) as far back as my mid-teens. However, at the age of 12, I experienced the trauma of being diagnosed with Type 1 Diabetes and then, at the age of 15, I was involved in a car accident. I awoke from a nap to discover that we were driving the wrong way up the M6 towing our overturned caravan behind us. It was a miracle that we didn't have a collision with other vehicles. So, was Bipolar Disorder always with me or were the traumas I experienced the catalyst for the mood disorder? Who knows?

My personal experience of living with PTSD is that I needed a multi-faceted approach in order to recover. Medication did help but, for me, it was the therapies and the implementation of the strategies I learned during therapy that made a significant difference to my life. It was my fervent hope that I could get better and that my constant state of anxiety would fade that motivated me to get my life back. On reflection, learning that I could alter my thoughts and manage my anxiety was empowering and any successes, however small, spurred me on to explore other options with an open mind. I have the NHS and myself to thank for that approach - but the journey on which I embarked was totally driven by me.

Mood

(Noun: a temporary state of mind or feeling) (*Oxford English Dictionary*)

In simple terms, the concept of mood in clinical psychology comes from the analysis of emotion. It is obviously much more complicated than that simplified statement and can be difficult to define. We often refer to a person as being "in a mood" but that's different to their state of mood, that is, where they are emotionally. Moods can fluctuate quickly which differentiates them from a person's temperament or their personality traits, both of which are longer lasting and less changeable. A person's state of mood can be less specific and more intense. We often talk about mood in terms of it being good or bad but it's much more subjective than that and our interpretation of our own mood, and that of others, is heavily influenced by our own life experiences. Mood is on a spectrum and can be influenced by many factors, including the following:

Sleep

Sleep deprivation is considered a form of torture. This is unsurprising as so much internal regulation occurs within the body whilst we sleep. The body repairs cells, restores energy and releases hormones such as Melatonin which not only controls the sleep-wake cycle but is also the growth hormone that helps the body self-heal. Just one night's bad sleep can affect mood and I'm sure we all can relate to that.

Environment

Your environment has an enormous impact on your mood. This can encompass many distinct aspects of your life such as your housing environment, family situation, work environment and "the environment" in terms of the time spent outside and enjoying time in nature. If your environment is having a negative impact on your mood, simple, small changes can make a significant and noticeable difference.

The seasons also can negatively impact mood with the long dark days and lack of sunlight during the winter months causing seasonal depression. This is known as Seasonal Affective Disorder ("SAD") and is characterised by persistent low mood. The condition is not fully understood although the following factors are believed to have a significant influence:

- lack of exposure to sunlight which may cause a part of the brain known as the hypothalamus to stop functioning optimally;
- higher levels of melatonin causing sleepiness;
- lower serotonin levels causing changes to mood, appetite and sleep; and
- an alteration in the body's natural rhythm also called the Circadian Rhythm due to the lack of sunlight. This causes your sleep/wake cycle to be disrupted and you sleep too much or too little.

Nutrition

The hormone serotonin is a “chemical messenger” which acts as a mood stabiliser. Up to 90% of serotonin is produced in the gut! 90%! Wow! So, obviously, having good gut health and investing time in eating healthily will have an impact on mood. The opposite is also true as eating poorly will reduce the body’s ability to produce serotonin and will lead to lower mood.

Alongside nutrition sits hydration. Drinking plenty of water and/or getting it through other sources, such as fruit and vegetables, is also vital for stabilising mood.

Hormones

Although the phrase “I’m so hormonal” is attributed to women, hormones affect both males and females. Many hormones, including serotonin and melatonin, regulate bodily functions such as growth, metabolism, sexual function, reproduction and mood. They stabilise the body but, if a hormonal imbalance occurs, mood may change.

Drugs and alcohol

The use of illicit drugs, abuse of prescription drugs and/or alcohol abuse may also affect mood both in the short term and longer term. The use of some illicit drugs is known to cause mental illness. Of course, the side effects of some prescribed medications can also have a positive or negative effect on mood.

Everyone has fluctuations in their mood and some may even describe themselves as having mood swings. This is completely normal unless changes in your mood disrupt your life or the lives of those around you.

Extremes of mood, both severely negative "Dysphoria" and extremely positive "Euphoria", are signs that something is amiss with your mental health and you should ask for help from your GP.

Dysphoria: a constant state of profound unhappiness and dissatisfaction.

Symptoms: hopelessness, lethargy, lack of appetite or binge eating, sleep disruption either too much or too little, lack of interest in usual activities, low self-esteem, inability to care for oneself and lack of positive emotions.

Euphoria: a feeling of intense elation and happiness that's more than reasonable in a particular situation.

Symptoms: heightened joy, exaggerated optimism, rapid thoughts, restlessness and inflated self-esteem.

www.verywellhealth.com

Mood Disorders

The most common mood disorders are:

- ***Bipolar disorder***: periods of depression alternating with periods of hypomania or mania. Lots more on this, just read on.
- ***Dysthymia***: chronic depressed mood lasting for at least two years.
- ***Major depression***: depression symptoms lasting for at least two weeks.
- ***Mood disorder related to another condition***: medical illness such as cancer can trigger symptoms of depression.

- ***Substance-induced mood disorder***: depression symptoms due to effects of medication, drug or alcohol abuse or exposure to toxins.
- ***Drug-induced psychosis***: psychosis is when a person loses contact with reality. Symptoms may include hallucinations and delusions. The use of certain illegal drugs including cannabis and cocaine can induce psychosis.
- ***Postpartum depression and postpartum psychosis***: extremely low or high mood after giving birth.

My personal experience of Mood

I've experienced extremes of high and low mood and, occasionally, a mixed state with feelings of a high mood whilst also experiencing depression symptoms. In the beginning, I could justify how I was feeling and the reasons for my mood. As the extremes widened and began to impact my life, I reached out for help from my GP. Like most people who are experiencing a range of moods that are impacting their ability to function properly, I went to see my doctor when my mood was low. It made no sense to see my GP when I was extremely happy and could multi-task a hundred things at once!

There is currently a campaign encouraging GPs to ask patients to complete a short, two-minute bipolar questionnaire when they present with depression symptoms. This would help with early identification of people with mood disorders. The average diagnosis time for someone with bipolar disorder is nine and a half years (Bipolar UK).

For me, it took 17 years for a diagnosis. It wasn't until my elevated mood was creating absolute havoc for me and my family that they called an intervention and took me to the GP. I wasn't sleeping or eating, I was paranoid, my thoughts were rapid and my behaviour was reckless and totally out of character. Now, my mood is relatively stable but keeping it within normal levels requires daily monitoring. I'm constantly checking in with myself and my family also keep a close eye on me. Knowing and responding to particular triggers, having a good routine and responding to subtle mood changes early are vital in balancing my mood.

Bipolar Disorder

The term "bipolar disorder" was first used in 1980. It replaced the term "manic depression" which was linked to sufferers being labelled as maniacs which brought additional stigma. Sometimes, I still hear the phrase "manic depression" and understand that people may be unaware that it's the same as bipolar disorder. But what actually is it? It's a mood disorder and the "bi" part of the word refers to two as people with the condition can experience two extremes of mood; mania where they feel very high and overactive, and depression where their mood is low and they lack motivation. The "polar" part of the word refers to extremes.

There are several types of bipolar disorder:

- **Bipolar 1** - characterised by moods shifting across the full mood scale from depressive to manic states. Diagnosis of this type of bipolar follows at least one episode of mania lasting over one week and 90% of these people will also have suffered depressive episodes.
- **Bipolar 2** - characterised by episodes of severe depression and at least one episode of hypomania (the stage before full mania). Symptoms include elevated self-esteem, everything

in excess (spending, talking, taking on new projects), rapid thoughts and speech.

- **Bipolar 1 or 2 with mixed features** - often referred to as "mixed bipolar state" where symptoms of hypomania and depression occur at the same time.
- **Bipolar 1 or 2 with rapid cycling** - rapid cycling is the term used when someone experiences four or more depressive, manic or hypomanic episodes over the course of twelve months.
- **Bipolar 1 or 2 seasonal pattern** - where the state of the person's mood is affected by the seasons. It may be that winter is more likely to be linked to depressive episodes although hypomania/mania may not follow a pattern. This is different to Seasonal Affective Disorder ("SAD") as sufferers of that condition are only affected in the winter and don't experience feelings of hypomania or mania whereas bipolar disorder sufferers can be affected any time and also experience feelings of hypomania or mania.
- **Cyclothymia** - regular episodes of hypomania and depression that last over two years; there will be no period longer than two months where the mood is stable and no episodes of mixed states.
- **Psychosis** - severe mania or severe depression may be accompanied by periods of psychosis where the person may suffer hallucinations and/or delusions.

  Hallucinations are when a person hears, sees, smells, tastes or feels things that appear real but only exist in their mind.

Delusions are an unshakeable belief in something that is untrue. These can include delusions of grandeur where a person thinks they can control the weather or thinks that they are a very important person or religious figure.

As you can see, even within the umbrella term "bipolar disorder", there are different variations of the condition, and a wide range of symptoms and the condition may present differently in each individual. It can be frightening to experience such distinct moods especially when symptoms can alter so quickly and manifest in different ways or when multiple symptoms are experienced simultaneously.

I was diagnosed with "cyclothymia", sometimes referred to as "mild bipolar disorder". For me, the term "mild" totally misrepresents my experience. I have found that psychiatrists have different views on the term with some referring to it as "cyclothymia" and others just calling it "bipolar". Personally, I find that identifying myself as a person with bipolar disorder reflects my symptoms as I have experienced everything on the Bipolar UK mood scale from 0 *severe depression* to 9 *mania*. Whilst a label can be useful (especially for me in terms of finding the right medication), I've also tried to focus on, and find ways to manage, my symptoms and difficulties.

The Bipolar Mood Scale

Ideally, you are aiming to be in the middle/green area of the mood scale. This is where mood is balanced and emotions are relative to the experiences you are having. Yellow areas are cause for concern as mood is becoming unstable but, if interventions are put in place at this point, mood can be regulated again without further de-escalation/escalation.

If mood is coming into the red areas, this is cause for significant concern and medical intervention is needed. Below is a copy of the Bipolar UK Mood Scale.

bipolar UK Mood Scale

SUPPORTING PEOPLE AFFECTED BY BIPOLAR

This scale is not meant to be definitive but is an indicator of possible behaviours

Mania	10	Total loss of judgement, exorbitant spending, religious delusions and hallucinations.
	9	Lost touch with reality, incoherent, no sleep, paranoid and vindictive, reckless behaviour.
Hypomania	8	Inflated self-esteem, rapid thoughts and speech, counter-productive simultaneous tasks.
	7	Very productive, everything to excess (phone calls, writing, smoking, tea), charming and talkative.
Balanced Mood	6	Self-esteem good, optimistic, sociable and articulate, good decisions and get work done.
	5	Mood in balance, no symptoms of depression or mania. Life is going well and the outlook is good.
	4	Slight withdrawal from social situations, concentration less than usual, slight agitation.
Mild to Moderate Depression	3	Feelings of panic and anxiety, concentration difficult and memory poor, some comfort in routine.
	2	Slow thinking, no appetite, need to be alone, sleep excessive or difficult, everything a struggle.
Severe Depression	1	Feelings of hopelessness and guilt, thoughts of suicide, little movement, impossible to do anything.
	0	Endless suicidal thoughts, no way out, no movement, everything is bleak and it will always be like this.

In the early days, after I was diagnosed, I used this mood scale daily along with a mood diary. It was essential for me to know what was happening in my life at any given time so I collected data on sleep, medication, diet, activities and changes from my normal routine as this enabled me to begin observing things that were triggering changes and causing my mood to elevate or decrease. Once I had this knowledge, I was able to start developing strategies and intervening before my mood changed.

Treatments

A combination of one or more of these can be used.

- Medication may be prescribed to prevent episodes of mania and depression. This type of medication is called a mood stabiliser and is taken daily on a long-term basis. Medication can also be prescribed during episodes of mania or depression for the duration of the bipolar episode.
- Developing self-awareness of the condition by using diaries or journals; identifying triggers and signs of approaching manic or depressive episodes to prevent them from occurring by using self-help strategies.
- Paper-based or online mood trackers are available. The Bipolar UK mood tracker app is excellent.
- Psychological treatment e.g. talking therapies to help in dealing with depression, feelings of guilt and shame following manic episodes and to help improve relationships.
- Lifestyle choices e.g. routine, regular exercise, sleep programme, improved diet and reduction of caffeine and/or alcohol intake.

Depression

Anyone can experience low mood or feeling down but these feelings will pass in a few days and are usually linked to a specific event or reason. Depression is when these symptoms last for more than two weeks and can last for many months. Symptoms may vary in intensity. Milder symptoms will allow the person to continue with their daily life and routines whereas severe symptoms can affect every aspect of their life.

Causes of Depression

There's a wide range of reasons someone may be suffering from depression. Women are more likely to be diagnosed than men but this may be because men are less likely to seek help when experiencing symptoms. The LGBTQI community also display higher rates of depression.

There is a wide range of things that may trigger depression but it can also occur without an obvious cause. These include:

- Childhood trauma and experiences;
- Life events including loss, grief, abuse and trauma;
- Existing mental health problems;
- Physical health issues including illness and injury or pain;
- Family history of depression;
- Medication side effects;
- The use of recreational drugs and alcohol;
- Sleep disturbances;
- Diet/poor nutrition;
- Exercise, especially a lack of.

Symptoms of Depression

Depression has an impact on the way a person feels and also on the way they behave or act.

Feelings:

- Sad, upset or tearful;
- Restlessness and agitation;
- Worthlessness or lack of self-esteem;
- Numbness or feeling a lack of emotion;
- Lack of pleasure in things you normally enjoy;
- Anger;
- Frustration;
- Lack of confidence;
- Hopelessness;
- Fatigue;
- Suicidal thoughts.

Behaviour:

- Avoiding social events or hobbies they are usually fond of;
- Self-harm;
- Unable to speak clearly or make decisions;
- Loss of libido;
- Lack of concentration;
- Inability to remember things;
- Increased use of tobacco, alcohol or drugs;
- Difficulty sleeping – either too little or too much;

- Lack of appetite resulting in weight loss;
- Increased appetite resulting in weight gain;
- Physical aches and pains with no apparent reason;
- Moving slowly;
- Restlessness.

Types of depression

Persistent depressive disorder: continuous symptoms of depression for two years or more.

Seasonal affective disorder: depression that occurs at a particular time of year and is often associated with winter.

Antenatal depression: depression that occurs during pregnancy.

Postnatal depression: depression that occurs in the first year after a pregnancy. This can also affect fathers or partners.

Premenstrual dysphoric disorder: a hormone-related disorder linked to menstruation that affects how a person feels physically and mentally.

Treatments for Depression

Medication in the form of antidepressants, or psychotherapy, is commonly used to treat depression. Treatments also include talking therapies such as CBT or counselling; self-help can be very useful and there are lots of free resources available online; involvement in hobbies or creative outlets and increasing exercise and time outdoors are helpful.

Anxiety

Anxiety is a feeling of worry, nervousness, unease and apprehension. Occasional anxiety is a regular occurrence in normal life and has always been part of the human experience. Anxiety disorders, however, involve more than temporary nervousness and fear. Anxiety does not go away and over time can worsen.

Types of Anxiety Disorder

Generalised anxiety disorder: sufferers have regular and often uncontrollable worries linked to everyday occurrences.

Social anxiety disorder: anxiety is caused by social situations; this can include school, work, shops, parties, etc.

Panic disorder: sufferers experience regular or frequent panic attacks (an exaggeration of the body's typical response to danger, stress or excitement): see below for more information.

Phobias: an extreme fear or anxiety that is triggered by something specific e.g. spiders, flying, etc.

Post Traumatic Stress Disorder (PTSD): anxiety caused as part of a response to a traumatic event.

Obsessive Compulsive Disorder (OCD): anxiety combined with repetitive thoughts, impulsive behaviour and compulsions.

Health anxiety: when someone spends a lot of time worrying that they are ill or going to become ill. This can be related to OCD.

Body dysmorphic disorder (BDD): when someone experiences obsessions and negative thoughts about their appearance.

Perinatal anxiety: develops during pregnancy or during the first year after giving birth.

Panic Attacks

Panic attacks are a type of fear response. They can come on suddenly and can be frightening. People who experience them say they feel like they are losing control and they may feel like they are having a heart attack or may die. It is very unpleasant.

What do panic attacks feel like?

The symptoms of a panic attack are felt physically in the body.

- Palpitations – a pounding heart;
- Feelings of faintness, dizziness or light-headedness;
- Changes in temperature – too hot or too cold;
- Sweating trembling or shaking;
- Pain or tightness in the chest or stomach;
- Struggling to catch breath;
- Feelings of choking;
- Feeling wobbly or shaky, especially in the legs;
- Feeling disconnected from the mind, body or surroundings. This is often referred to as dissociation..

The following can cause anxiety:

- Childhood trauma or experiences;
- Current issues in your life;
- Physical and/or mental health issues;
- Drugs and medication.

Treatment

As with all mental health conditions, there are a variety of treatment options. Usually, a combination of treatments is used; for example, medication with talking therapies and self-help with peer support can be valuable in treating the cause of the anxiety not just the symptoms.

Psychosis

Psychosis refers to a range of symptoms affecting the mind, specifically where a loss of contact with reality is experienced. A person will experience disruption to their thoughts and perceptions and they may be unable to recognise what is and isn't real. Psychosis can affect people in different ways. It may be experienced just once as an isolated episode, multiple short episodes throughout their life or they may live with it most of the time.

It's difficult to provide an accurate statistic as to how many people experience psychosis. Research has estimated between 15 and 100 people out of 100,000 develop psychosis each year (National Institute of Mental Health).

Types of psychosis

Hallucinations

This includes seeing things that other people don't see (faces, animals or religious figures), seeing objects that appear distorted or move abnormally, and experiencing sensory occurrences and sensations such as tastes, smells and tactile disturbances, for example, feeling like insects are crawling on your skin.

People may also experience auditory hallucinations or hear voices no one else can hear and these voices may be positive or negative.

Delusions

People suffering from psychosis typically experience delusions which are also called false beliefs. These feel completely real to the person suffering from psychosis but there is no evidence to back these things up as existing in reality to other people.

Some people experience a symptom called “delusions of grandeur” which is when the person feels they have the power to alter things such as the weather, cure cancer or end wars, or that they are a very important person. Someone suffering from delusions may also spend a lot of money or get themselves into debt due to their sense of reality being affected.

A sub-type of delusion is paranoid delusion where a person feels threatened and at risk; they may feel unsafe and that someone is going to hurt or kill them even though the threat doesn’t exist.

Disorganised thinking and speaking

Disorganised thinking, also referred to as “Formal Thought Disorder”, can also be a specific type of psychosis. This is split into two sections. **Racing thoughts** which is literally as it’s named, thoughts racing through the person’s head very quickly and feeling out of control. **Flight of ideas** which is where thoughts move quickly through the person’s mind. The thoughts are unrelated to each other and flit from one thing to another but, to the person suffering from psychosis, they seem connected and they find links between them. This can present as talking very fast, stumbling over words, jumbled speech, talking about lots of unconnected topics one after the other and the inability to hold focus on one topic.

Disordered thinking and speaking can also be a symptom of bipolar disorder during hypomanic or manic episodes. This could be without other symptoms of psychosis, although psychosis can also occur in bipolar disorder.

Signs and symptoms of psychosis

The following changes in behaviour can be signs a person is entering or suffering psychosis:

- Paranoia;
- Inability to think clearly or logically;
- Social withdrawal and increased time alone;
- Having intense ideas, unusual feelings or lack of emotion;
- Not looking after themselves properly, lack of self-care and personal hygiene;
- Disrupted sleep;
- Inability to tell the difference between reality and fantasy;
- Trouble speaking or communicating;
- Changes in productivity at work or school;
- Behaving in unpredictable ways;
- Self-harming;
- Threatening or aggressive behaviour.

Is psychosis a symptom or a diagnosis?

The term psychosis refers to an experience, a person will often be described as experiencing psychosis as it is a symptom related to certain mental health conditions rather than a condition in its own right. Psychosis can be experienced on its own and as an isolated episode, being referred to brief psychotic disorder.

Psychosis is linked to the following conditions:

- Severe depression;
- Schizophrenia;
- Bipolar disorder;
- Schizoaffective disorder;
- Paranoid personality disorder;
- Postpartum depression psychosis;
- Delusional disorder.

Causes of psychosis

It isn't always easy to identify the causes of a psychotic episode. However, contributing factors may include:

- Injury or illness;
- Abuse or trauma;
- Use of illegal drugs;
- Alcohol;
- Smoking;
- Prescription medication;
- Coming off psychiatric drugs;
- Hunger or low blood sugars;

- Lack of sleep;
- Bereavement;
- Spiritual experiences;
- Genetic inheritance.

MIND– mental health charity

Treatments for psychosis

The main treatment offered is antipsychotic medication, other medications used include antidepressants and mood stabilisers. A range of therapies may be offered including talking therapies, CBT or a specialised variation of this called CBTp Cognitive Behavioural Therapy for Psychosis, art therapy to help with the expression of feelings that the person may be unable to talk about and family intervention which facilitates talking together and problem-solving as a couple or family.

I have
overcome
many things

Traditional Mental Health Treatments

Medication

There are a variety of different medication options available for people who have bipolar disorder.

Mood stabilisers

Lithium is the most common medication prescribed for bipolar disorder. It's used to treat episodes of mania, hypomania and regular periods of depression where other medications have not been successful. Once lithium is prescribed, its dose is slowly increased and the user has regular blood tests until the correct level is established; these tests are required every three months to ensure the level of lithium isn't too high which can cause lithium toxicity, a very serious condition.

Lithium toxicity occurs if the medication dose is too high or it can be caused by dehydration. Symptoms include vomiting, visual disturbances, confusion, blackouts, slurred speech, excessive thirst, bladder and bowel incontinence and shaking including spasms, twitching or jerking. The kidneys, gastrointestinal tract and central nervous system are affected. Early treatment is essential to prevent further symptoms such as coma, seizures and heart problems including heart attacks.

There's a long list of side effects with lithium so blood tests are also done to check thyroid and kidney function and regular electrocardiographs/ECGs may be done to check the heart. Lithium also interacts with many other medications so it's vital that people prescribed lithium only take other medications prescribed by a doctor or over-the-counter medication that's been checked by a pharmacist. There are different brands of lithium and, once you are prescribed a particular brand, you must only ever use that brand because different brands can be absorbed differently, changing the level of lithium in the blood.

Anticonvulsants

Anticonvulsants may also be used as mood stabilisers, including carbamazepine, lamotrigine and valproate. Anticonvulsants work by calming hyperactivity in the brain and are often prescribed for people with rapid cycling. They can be used alone or in combination with lithium or an antipsychotic medication.

Antipsychotics

Antipsychotics are another type of medication used to treat bipolar disorder. The NICE guidelines (Antipsychotics | Prescribing information | Bipolar disorder | CKS | NICE) recommended the following medications for use in treating bipolar disorder:

- haloperidol – also known as Dozic, Haldol, Haldol Decanoate, Serenace;
- olanzapine – also known as Zalasta, Zyprexa, ZypAdhera;
- quetiapine – also known as Atrolak, Biquelle, Ebesque, Seroquel, Tenprolide, Zaluron;
- risperidone – also known as Risperdal, Risperdal Consta.

Antipsychotics can help reduce symptoms of psychosis. They can help control the following aspects of bipolar disorder:

- Anxiety and agitation;
- Confusion;
- Delusions and hallucinations including paranoia and hearing voices;

- Mania and hypomania;
- Violent or disruptive behaviour.

Antipsychotics can also reduce the likelihood of these symptoms recurring.

So how do antipsychotics actually work? They work by blocking the action of dopamine in the brain; too much dopamine means messages in the brain are passed from one nerve cell to another too quickly. The antipsychotic drug slows the flow of the messages in turn reducing the bipolar symptoms.

They also work by affecting brain chemicals; chemicals in the brain known as neurotransmitters such as glutamate, noradrenaline and serotonin which are important in regulating your mood and antipsychotics can help to regulate the levels of these chemicals.

Antidepressants ARE NOT mood stabilisers; they fall into a separate category of psychiatric medication. People with bipolar disorder who are prescribed antidepressants may experience hypomania or mania as the medication lifts their mood too much. This happened to me when I first went to my GP with depression and PTSD symptoms and was prescribed an antidepressant which caused rapid cycling.

For more information on the different medications and options for treating bipolar disorder, you can check out the following websites.

www.bipolaruk.org
www.NHS.uk
www.Mind.Org.uk

Therapy

There are lots of different therapy options available for people with bipolar disorder. Some of these will be available on the NHS but are usually time-limited to a specific number of sessions or you can access them privately. This is particularly relevant to talking therapies; however, there is also a wide variety of complimentary therapies that can be accessed privately which may support recovery and maintaining a balanced mood. It's important to have a good rapport with your therapist and sometimes, if this isn't the case, you may have to try someone or something else. This doesn't mean therapy isn't an excellent tool to use. It is but, if the therapist isn't the right fit for you, then you should try again. Don't give up! All therapists have a duty of care. Your sessions will remain confidential unless your therapist thinks you are going to harm yourself or someone else. In these circumstances, they are required to share this information. This is a legal requirement.

Here are some of the therapies available. Not all of these are specifically used for people with bipolar disorder but, as our life experiences are unique, I felt it would be helpful to have a wider overview of the support that's available.

Addiction Treatment

In some cases, mood disorders including bipolar disorder can be induced by alcohol or drug misuse. Dealing with the root of the problem will be vital to stabilise your mood. Lots of behaviours in bipolar disorder can become addictive and lead to difficulty in stopping even when the current mood changes. For example, overspending can be a symptom of hypomania and mania so it may be that help and support are required with this specific element of the condition. It may be that inpatient or outpatient rehabilitation is required which is intensive support, going through a detoxification process which may require medication to ease the severity of withdrawal symptoms. Support groups and CBT or DBT, which is used to help people who experience emotions very intensely, can also be useful.

It is recommended that you find a psychologist who specialises in addiction to work through the reasons why this has occurred and to have 1:1 support to create a treatment plan.

CBT

Cognitive Behavioural Therapy (CBT) is a talking therapy which is based on the concept that thoughts, feelings, actions and sensations in your body are all associated. Negative thoughts and feelings can make you feel trapped in a negative spiral.

CBT is often used to treat anxiety and depression. It deals with the issues you are currently dealing with, as opposed to other types of therapy that focus on past trauma and issues. It's an effective way to treat a wide range of mental health conditions and aims to teach you skills and techniques that you can use in your daily life by providing you with the tools needed to make an impact on your life long after your CBT sessions have ended. If you commit to using these learned skills in your life, it can have a big impact in a relatively short time.

Counselling

Counselling is also a talking therapy that is used to help address problems. A counsellor will support you and help you to gain better self-awareness, develop practical strategies to tackle your issues and explore different options available to you.

During a session, you will be encouraged to share your feelings and emotions so that the counsellor can get to know you and your way of thinking. They will also guide you to finding solutions for yourself.

Counsellors are specially trained and the issues that people seek counselling for include abuse (physical, emotional, domestic, financial and sexual abuse), childhood trauma, addiction, communication and relationship issues, grief, parenting, self-esteem, stress, anxiety and depression, sexuality, trauma and work-related issues.

DBT

Dialectical Behaviour Therapy (DBT) is another talking therapy which is based on CBT but it's been specially adapted to support people suffering from very intense emotions, often those diagnosed with mood disorders or personality disorders. This therapy may be carried out in a group setting. CBT deals with learning to change negative thoughts whereas DBT is focused on accepting thoughts. CBT is useful for those suffering from depression or anxiety while DBT is more useful for those with borderline personality disorder, bipolar disorder and chronic suicidal ideation.

DBT helps you to change your thought processes and provides you with a range of skills and techniques to try. Originally developed to support people with personality disorders, it's also used to help people who self-harm, experience suicidal thoughts or attempts and severe depression. DBT can be very effective if you engage with the process and are dedicated to making changes in your life.

There are two main aspects of DBT: acceptance techniques and change techniques. This means that you gain insight into who you are as a person and why you choose to use certain coping mechanisms and then you then learn alternative ways to deal with distress and how to challenge unhelpful thought patterns and make them more positive. DBT is available for children and adults.

EMDR

Eye Movement Desensitisation Reprocessing (EMDR) is used primarily to work with people who have experienced trauma. It can also be used for anxiety, depression, low self-esteem and phobias. EMDR works by processing the trauma; you are asked to recall the trauma over and over whilst receiving "bilateral sensory input". This can take the form of following lights or an object from left to right and back again, tracking it with your eyes, or hand tapping or hearing tones. You will be guided through some relaxation techniques to use before, during and after the sessions as going into your trauma is obviously very distressing. After putting yourself into the trauma and following the movement, you will be asked to think about the trauma again and see how it feels. This process is repeated until your thoughts and feelings are more positive and you can recall the traumatic event without experiencing negative physical and emotional feelings.

Family Therapy

Family therapy is exactly what it sounds like. A couple or family, including children, work with a therapist to develop better communication and listening skills and change the way issues are tackled to resolve conflicts and improve relationships. The NHS Community Mental Health Teams provide the sessions which last for between 60 and 90 minutes.

There may be one or two therapists present. Each person gets a chance to share their views and be listened to. Then the therapist will support the family to come up with workable solutions to deal with difficult situations.

After the session, the couple or family can work on the solutions and then feedback at the next session. Sessions are fortnightly or monthly and the family will be seen twelve times in total.

Peer Support

Now, this is a big category as peer support can take many guises. Peer support is when someone with a shared experience, i.e. has faced what you are facing, can offer support. This could be a friend or family member who has experienced mental health issues, a support group or a 1:1 session. As the person offering support knows what it's like to experience similar issues, they can share what they have been through and the different strategies they found helpful.

Knowing you are not alone, and that you can do things that can help you, has a huge impact. No one is told what to do; each person listens to the other person share their experiences and the things they have found that helped. With this information, the person receiving the support can choose whether to try some of the techniques they have heard about or consider other things that may have occurred to them during the time they have spent at the session.

Peer support can also take place online in forums or on social media platforms where people share their journeys and offer support. This method of support can be quite informal, making it easier to access for some people.

Psycho-sexual Therapy

Psychosexual therapy is a method of targeted counselling that is used to focus on sexual problems. It's another talking therapy as the problems are emotional and psychological.

I've included it here because hypersexuality is a symptom of hypomania and mania and can cause relationship issues as a result of adultery, inability to reach sexual climax and, on the other end of the spectrum, depression can cause loss of libido.

My Therapy

I wouldn't be where I am today without the help of various therapies and therapists. Some therapies have followed a very medical model and I've either paid privately or I've had support on the NHS. Today, my therapy takes a very different form. It's probably not "therapy" as you would automatically think of it. It's about being surrounded by like-minded people who are compassionate, caring and great at both listening and sharing their journeys with me and this form of therapy is definitely helping me with my personal growth, awareness and healing. Plenty more of that later!

Once I was diagnosed with PTSD, it was recommended that I should have EMDR therapy as part of the personal injury insurance claim I was undertaking. It was the psychiatrist from the insurance company who suggested it and I was given a list of possible therapists. The first sessions I had were paid for privately and, whilst they helped me to process the car accident from my teens and later when the coach hit our car, I think I was too unwell to truly benefit from it. Bear in mind that I hadn't been diagnosed with bipolar disorder at this stage and so my emotional state was too fragile for EMDR. I found it very difficult to cope would self-harm a lot in the hours that followed each session. The last private session I had was a few weeks before I was admitted to the psychiatric hospital.

A few years later, when the bipolar was a lot more stable, I was offered more EMDR on the NHS. My family were naturally very nervous as they felt the previous EMDR sessions had contributed to the severity of my symptoms. However, the psychologist was fantastic; she listened to my experience of the previous therapy and the signs that would indicate that a session should stop. We worked together at a slower pace, carefully monitoring my emotional state and behaviour after each session.

I was also supported by a mental health occupational therapist who started me on my mindfulness journey. We worked towards getting me back to work, rediscovering practical skills and rebuilding my self-confidence. I was referred to The Richmond Fellowship which is a mental health charity and their employment services supported me with meetings at work and also secured a place for me on a confidence-building course.

To be honest, I wasn't sure about attending the confidence-building course as, when I was hypomanic, I had confidence in spades and I felt I needed to learn to be less confident. However, when I was depressed, I felt a million miles away from the person I had been two years before. The confidence-building course was actually very good and I found myself surrounded by people who were experiencing similar feelings and emotions to me and there was no judgement. The best thing about the course was meeting Chris who was running it. He asked me, at the end of the course, if I would be interested in learning Reiki. I didn't really know what it was at that point. Chris was unsure if my Christian beliefs would be at odds with the Reiki practice but, the way I see it, God wants me to be well and to be the best version of myself and that involves me learning new skills. So, I embarked on my Reiki journey which has been so monumental in my recovery – so much so that I've dedicated an entire chapter to it!

I allow myself to feel whatever I need to

The Early Days

My recovery began when I was discharged from hospital. I had been diagnosed and had been prescribed lithium which is a mood stabiliser.

As I began to rebuild my life, I had no concept of who I was. I didn't recognise myself and was struggling terribly with feelings of shame and guilt over my uncharacteristic behaviour, mainly when I was manic but also when severe depression caused me to resort to self-harm. I was really lucky that my husband was able to take some time off work so when I came home from the hospital, I had him close by to monitor me and keep me safe.

I started my journey by completing small, achievable tasks and I quickly found that establishing a routine was really important. Just covering the basics was enough! I repeat <u>just covering the basics was enough</u>! It's too easy to try to do everything at once and then feel like a failure. I had to come to terms with the fact that I was really unwell and that getting washed and dressed, eating regular meals and taking the dog out for a walk was a lot for me to manage at that stage - and also enough. Having a dog and a child, who I had to get to school, was great for establishing a morning routine. There was a set timeframe in which I had to achieve certain tasks and I found that afterwards I would feel exhausted and needed to rest. I realised that rest is productive! If I needed to rest in the afternoon to build up the reserves I needed for the school pick up, afternoon dog walk and making tea, then I rested.

I was offered a course of DBT. This was a group session and, for me, it really helped to be with other people who understood how I felt. I left each session armed with useful strategies to help quieten that inner negative voice and manage my emotions.

I won't lie, I was still a long way off being stable but I was beginning to understand that I had the ability to influence and sometimes control my thoughts. I also had my first lessons in mindfulness which is such a huge topic that I've devoted an entire chapter to it later.

During DBT, I was given an information sheet entitled "Keeping Out of Emotional Mind" which included an acronym of the word **STRENGTH** and it was so useful to me that it remained pinned to my kitchen cupboard for years. I love it! A quick run-down of the list shows me immediately if something is a bit "wobbly". If I can identify what's not working, I can look at what needs to change or what requires more focus.

Emotional Mind

How to stay out of emotional mind

A way to remember these skills is to use the acronym:

S-T-R-E-N-G-T-H

Sleep

Take care of yourself

Resist unhelpful behaviours

Exercise

Nutrition

Gain mastery

Take time for yourself

Healthy self-talk

Sleep: practise healthy sleep habits. For example, if you have difficulty sleeping, avoid napping during the day and keep to a sleep programme. Creating a sleep routine, where you go to bed at the same time every evening and get up at the same time every morning, can be helpful. For an hour before bedtime, replace screens or devices with a calm, relaxing activity.

Take care of yourself: take care of your physical health. See a doctor when necessary and take medication as prescribed. Make looking after yourself a priority.

Resist unhelpful behaviours: avoid harmful activities and non-prescription drugs. Monitor your caffeine and alcohol intake. Harmful activities may include things like spending too much time on social media or accessing content on the internet that causes you anxiety or upset. Overspending and gambling also fall into this category.

Exercise: do some sort of exercise every day and try to build up to 20 minutes a day. This can be something simple like walking more, dancing in your kitchen or using a YouTube video at home. You may want to join a gym or exercise group and that's fine too.

Nutrition: eat foods that are good for you. Don't eat too much or too little. Stay away from foods that you know make you feel over-emotional; for example, highly processed or sugary foods can affect your mood causing anxiety and depression. Foods to Avoid If You Have Anxiety or Depression (webmd.com)

Gain Mastery: try to do at least one thing each day that makes you feel competent and in control. This may be something you are already skilful at such as playing an instrument or a creative outlet such as painting or sewing. Alternatively, you may be honing a new talent and this involves an investment in yourself. Often these activities are something you can lose yourself in.

Take Time For Yourself: each day, do something that you find relaxing, enjoyable or fun. Spend time in nature, chat to a friend, read, bake, draw; the possibilities are endless.

Healthy Self-talk: treat yourself with respect. Notice your positive qualities and your achievements, however small. Encourage yourself. Identify the times when you are negative toward yourself, challenge this habit and replace negative thoughts with positive ones.

(Source unknown)

Create a Safe Space

I was also taught a technique called "safe space". This is a visualisation technique to help with anxiety and panic attacks. Here's a step-by-step guide of how to create your own safe space.

1. Think of a place - mine is a real place on the West Pennine Moors where I used to go as a child. You could choose a real or imagined place - perhaps a forest, beach, under the sea or outer space.

2. Think of a word linked to your safe space - I chose the colour green.

3. Imagine yourself in your safe space - you can be doing anything you want. I imagine myself walking into my space very slowly, lying down on the grass and, after the visualisation process, I imagine I'm sitting up.

4. Now focus on what you can see in the space - for me, it's grass and rock, moss, clover leaves and flowers. Then animals

appear around me; deer, sheep, foxes, rabbits, butterflies, etc. I watch the shape of the clouds and their movement across the sky. It becomes a complete fantasy - not at all like reality. I'm transformed into Snow White with all the animals tamed and surrounding me.

5. Move on to focusing on your sense of hearing. What sounds can you hear in your safe space? Are the sounds loud or quiet, soft or harsh?

6. Next, focus on your sense of smell. For me, it's all the smells of nature including the smell of sheep poo which actually comes from my memory of visiting this place.

7. What can you touch in the space? If I'm lying on the grass, I sense which parts of my body are touching the earth. I reach out my fingertips and feel the grass, moss and pebbles.

8. In some safe spaces, it may feel appropriate to have some food or taste things such as the foods at a picnic, the saltiness of the sea or an ice cream.

The purpose of the safe space technique is to totally immerse yourself in that place in your mind. Like all mindfulness practices, your mind may wander and you might find yourself thinking about what you're having for tea that night. That's totally fine and exactly what minds do; everyone's mind does this. When you notice that your mind has wandered, simply bring yourself back into your safe place.

As I mentioned earlier, I have devoted an entire chapter to mindfulness where I explore this in more depth and provide some more ideas for you to try.

I'm not the person I was but I'm becoming the person I'm meant to be

Chronic Illness

We are never just one thing. We are complicated beings and the world around us is constantly changing and throwing challenges our way. I not only have to deal with balancing my bipolar disorder but also other concerns. In fact, often bipolar disorder is the least of my worries.

On 22 May 1993, when I was 12, I was diagnosed with Type 1 diabetes. It's only in the last few months that I've had an epiphany of just how traumatic that actually was for me, not only in terms of my physical health as my pancreas packed in but also in terms of the mental strain. In my case, that initial mental strain then turned into mental strength, resilience and determination mixed in with some downright stubbornness!

I have a vivid memory of the morning after I had been admitted to the hospital. I was sitting on the side of my hospital bed and in my hand was a syringe full of insulin. Before me stood an unsympathetic nurse (why she was working in the children's ward is a mystery to me) who told me to just give myself the injection. Somehow, I managed it although my eyes were so full of tears I couldn't see what I was doing. On reflection, I couldn't understand why my mum or dad weren't there with me for that first injection. It was a huge undertaking for me at such a young age and I needed to be surrounded by compassion and support.

Until recently, I referred to taking daily medication, blood tests and injections (over 75,000 in my life so far) as part of my daily grind. However, I came to realise that these were actually vitally important self-care practices. I've recently given my diet a dramatic overhaul by following the "Autoimmune Protocol Diet" which has improved my diabetic control. In turn, I have realised that other factors, over and above my bipolar symptoms, are responsible for making me feel physically and mentally unwell. By relabelling "daily grind" as "self-care", these practices have taken on an entirely new meaning in my life and are now prioritised as nurture rather than a nuisance.

I've also learned to use this technique in other settings. During a women's retreat, the facilitator of a particular session talked about dedicating tasks to women who didn't have the privileges that we had and it really resonated with me! Now, when I spend an hour cooking to feed my family and then do the dishes, it's not a drag - it's a privilege, especially when you consider that there are families, potentially in your neighbourhood or in a third-world country, struggling to survive. I know that I take many things completely for granted. I do still moan, and I do get grumpy because I'm only human after all but the ability to challenge my thoughts and redirect them from negative to positive is a skill I've practised and used in a wide range of settings and, the more I practise, the easier it becomes.

As I've said before, we are complicated beings and I often describe my health as complicated. Six years ago, at 2.00 am, I walked down the two flights of stairs from my bedroom to let Fudge out for a wee. This dog has the bladder of a camel and never needs a wee during the night. My antipsychotic meds make me very woozy and, as I started to walk down the second flight of stairs, I realised that my blood sugars were also low. I had taken only a couple of steps into my living room when my feet went from under me and I broke my leg in four places!

Since then, I've had surgery to place, and then to remove, a tibial nail into the entire length of my lower leg. I have experienced constant pain every waking minute of every day since I broke my leg, with no respite, no relief and no refrain. I've tried Reiki, acupuncture, Myo-skeletal massage, physio, yoga, swimming, Pilates, pain killers and nothing has helped. Absolutely nothing! Of all the health issues that I deal with, diabetes and bipolar disorder, this is by far the worst. I'm exhausted all the time; the pain dictates what I can and can't do and, because of it, I feel bitter and twisted at times, particularly when I'm struggling to drive any significant distance. I can't hop into the car to see my Mum or my Gran and it sucks. I'm angry and frustrated at my body but I'm also in absolute awe at what it can endure and still keep going.

Despite all my struggles, I have so much joy in my life. One thing that I'm eternally grateful for is hope. I have hope that I will find a solution to the things that are holding me back. My life experience provides evidence of this. I've never been dealt a hand I couldn't handle, I've never failed to use my mental resilience to guide me forward and I've never had a problem I couldn't tackle.

Medication doesn't work on its own

I'm currently on a combination of a mood stabiliser and an antipsychotic. The antipsychotic was added following my second manic episode and this combination has worked well for me for many years. There are side effects to manage and contend with but they are preferable to the catastrophic consequences of mania or the deep despair of depression.

I truly believe that my medication doesn't work on its own and this book is devoted to everything I've found that keeps my mood stable. I don't do them consistently or all at the same time but I monitor my mood carefully and implement whatever strategy feels right at the time. Often, it's trial and error to discover what helps. This journey of exploration to find out what works and, equally important, doesn't work is far from over. I've been travelling my wellness journey for ten years now and, in the last year, I've discovered so many new things that have boosted my ability to manage my mental health. I will continue to seek out new strategies because, the more I have in my arsenal, the easier it becomes to choose a strategy to match the situation. I've also learned to trust my instinct in terms which strategy to choose. If I'm drawn towards a particular strategy, there's usually a good reason. However, I still question if my decision is being driven by instinct or by mood fluctuations. This can be very subtle but, as I continue to practise, my self-awareness improves.

The Bipolar Toolkit

The Bipolar Toolkit by Sarah Freeman is a free resource that's available on www.bipolar-lives.com It's a lengthy document but a brilliant one; it aims to help you to learn as much as you can about your bipolar disorder and to find ways to manage your mood. It guides you through how to chart your mood and create daily charts and, once you're doing this regularly, it helps you to identify triggers. This information, in turn, helps you to create a two-step wellness plan.

When I used this resource, I really took my time with it and worked in bite-sized chunks so I didn't become overwhelmed. It took months for me to complete but I was left with a comprehensive document that was helpful and easy to use.

The Wellness Plan

As its name suggests, this is a plan to help you keep well. It's based on four principles: self-reliance, personal responsibility, education about your condition and support from people you trust. It's highly personalised to work just for you.

Your wellness plan comes into play when you first detect symptoms. Then, with speedy intervention, you can prevent any significant rises or falls in your mood. I also used the wellness plan to identify the things that need to be consistent in my life such as prioritising sleep, taking medication as prescribed and on time, eating healthily and walking the dogs twice a day to provide routine, exercise and fresh air. The wellness plan also encourages me to implement the strategies that I've found over the years that help me manage my symptoms. I've become quite skilled at identifying what I need and putting it into place because I've increased the focus on the things that make me wobbly and I've tried lots of different strategies. This often happens automatically without thought now.

The plan also helps you to identify triggers for depression, hypomania and mania and it provides a list of common triggers but also plenty of space for you to add your own. It includes a host of early warning signs that I instantly recognised and it introduced me to a few things that made perfect sense but that I'd never realised before. I also asked my family to contribute to my wellness plan as they see things I don't. Common wellness strategies follow these lists so, if you're at the beginning of your journey and not sure what to try, you'll have a few ideas to start with.

The Wellness Plan also includes a treatment contract. This is basically a list of things that your nearest and dearest can put in place if you become too unwell to make these decisions for yourself. When you are of sound mind, you create a document that says things like, "My access to the internet can be restricted," "I won't have access to my car keys," "I won't have access to my bank card or online payments" - you get the idea.

Asking family and close friends for input in each section of the toolkit can be really useful and, when it's complete, you then share it with those same people to review and sign. This gives you peace of mind in that, should you become unwell, those who care about you the most can step in and put things in place to stop things from escalating further. Part of the contract will also include the contact details for your psychiatrist or other significant health professionals and advice on when they should be contacted. Although this document is specifically designed for people with bipolar disorder, it can be adapted easily to work for people with a variety of mental illnesses. If you’re struggling with depression, simply ignore the parts that refer to hypomania and mania. If you suffer from psychosis, then focus on the mania section as there will be some crossover.

Just create your own wellness plan and crisis contract using all the knowledge you have about yourself. After all, you know yourself better than anyone!

Just as it is!

In a right flap!

So, when I made a plan of what to include in this book, this wasn't in it! Like everyone else, I experience lots of unexpected stresses and try to get a good work-life balance, whilst dealing with multiple health conditions. I've realised that sharing my life as it is now, fully armed with strategies and techniques in my mental health toolbox will demonstrate to you how you can manage your own mental health issues and how you can make a difference to yourself and your nearest and dearest. I definitely don't have it all sussed but, with the learning I've done, I can identify stress earlier and do my best in that moment to make life easier for myself. In this, the first "Just As It Is" piece, you can see that I'm still a work in progress but what I am doing is learning, learning all the time, so that the next time life goes crazy or I feel I can't cope, I can be reflective and I can react.

I'm currently sitting on a train on the way to visit my Gran. This is the third train I've been on so far today - just one more to go. With so many changes plus a very traumatic experience of missing a train just before my bipolar diagnosis, my anxiety levels are definitely raised; a mixture of excitement at seeing my Gran but also the apprehension of the journey. As a general rule, I don't suffer too much travel anxiety on trains. I do find the prospect of changing trains daunting as, with two dodgy legs (I broke the right one in four places and then, four years later I broke my left ankle), I'm slower than I used to be and live with chronic pain.

So, here's what happened today. My train coming into Leeds for my first connection was held outside the station for ten minutes. I came in on Platform 17 and my next train was on Platform 1. Leeds Station is huge! I hobbled from one side of the station to the other only to find my next train was gone. I went back upstairs and spoke to a staff member who sent me back downstairs to find a staff member from the train company I was travelling with. Lots of waiting for lifts and up and down was wasting valuable minutes and my adrenaline was pumping. I was wearing a mask but seemed to be the only one in the station wearing one as this was at the tail end of the Covid pandemic. Breathing too fast and starting to panic, the tears were now falling as I couldn't see any staff.

I then saw a train heading directly to Edinburgh which would stop me having to change at York. The problem was that I couldn't get on it with the ticket I'd bought. Could I find a member of staff who worked for the right train company? No, I couldn't! Now the anxiety was taking over, the calm collected mind from before the trip that said "If there are any problems, just ask a member of staff, that's what they are there for" had gone as my thoughts spiralled negatively downwards. Eventually, I found someone to ask and they told me to go to the platform of the Edinburgh train and ask there. Why didn't I think to do that? It's so obvious when you think about it with a clear head.

As I got to the platform, the doors were locked and they were waving to say the train was ready to depart. I couldn't get on! So now I was gasping for breath, fighting back the tears and having real feelings of despair. The mask was off, I couldn't breathe with it on any more as it was making me feel claustrophobic. I should have .... Woah! Wait right there! I try hard to avoid the word "should" it just isn't helpful and invokes feelings of guilt and worthlessness. Think instead, if this happens again, what have I learned that could change this situation in the future?

So now, I was on the next Edinburgh-bound train, heading to where I wanted to be. I might have been a bit late but it was actually out of my control. I couldn't have predicted or prevented the train being held outside Leeds Station. So, all I could do was take away a valuable lesson; if I miss my connection in future, go to the platform of the next available train as that's where the staff will be and I will be in the right place rather than running around like a headless chicken.

I've learned lessons similar to this in the past such as, if your train is delayed, don't go to buy a drink as you don't know how long it will take and you might miss the train. And breathe, slow down your breath; if you're wearing a face mask, briefly take it off; and talk gently and compassionately to yourself. Taking a few seconds to think clearly instead of letting the panic take over and sometimes letting the tears fall as a release instead of fighting them back can be helpful.

I learn from my mistakes

Peer Support

Peer support is when people with a shared experience can support one another in a safe environment. It's a completely different experience to hear someone speak about how they are coping with their own mental health and what they have found that helps rather than being told what to do by a clinician. When I had Dialectical Behaviour Therapy, provided by the NHS, being in a group setting and knowing that I was not alone was extremely important to me. I also accessed group work when I was an inpatient.

I often refer to peer support as magical because, if you've never experienced it and then you find support from people who genuinely understand and "get it", it opens a door to recovery and empowers you to make changes that have a huge impact on your ability to recover or redress the balance of your mental illness, especially if it's incurable. In peer support, we talk from the 'I'. For example, "When I find it difficult to sleep, I listen to a podcast' as opposed to "If you can't sleep, you should listen to a podcast'. What helps me may or may not help you but, if you hear my solutions, it may spark an idea for you to try something different. The biggest thing here, in my opinion, is choice.

The psychologist I worked with for my EMDR therapy once said to me, "You always have a choice". This was in relation to a fast-approaching second manic episode. I could choose to engage or I could choose another path. On that occasion, I engaged and everything went AWOL again but her words left an impression on me. I do have a choice and only I can choose. It's the same concept as peer support. If everyone in the room tells you about something that helps them when they can't sleep, you have a list of ideas to try and you can choose which to try for yourself, all of them or none of them. You are the driving force in your recovery.

The most valuable peer support I've experienced has been from Leeds Mind. I originally called them to enquire about an Emotional Eating workshop I had seen advertised as I had very disordered eating during both my manic and depressive episodes and I felt that some support regarding this would help. Unfortunately, there wasn't enough interest in the workshop so it wasn't running at that time. I did, however, have a lovely chat with the lady who answered the phone, probably a volunteer, and she told me about two workshops that were running that I might find helpful. So, I signed up!

Leeds Mind

The first time I went to Leeds Mind for one of these workshops, my anxiety was through the roof. It was a new place, I didn't know where it was, how to get there, who would be there or what to expect. I really didn't need to be worried at all. I can't remember what the workshop was about but I found myself in a room of people who totally understood me and knew how I felt as they had felt or were feeling it too. The two facilitators were both volunteers (it's slightly different now in that one of the facilitators is always a member of staff) and one of them had bipolar disorder. How fantastic for me to see someone with the same diagnosis in this role sharing the techniques they had learned to manage their condition.

Then something amazing, scary and downright unexpected happened. During the lunch break, one of the facilitators asked me if I would like to do the training to become a facilitator! I was blown away by this and very politely declined, explaining I had just come for some support. I went home and mulled it over. I think what amazed me most was that someone could see potential in me, something I thought was gone forever. They believed that I could lead a group, be in a position of authority and organise a session. Now, don't get me wrong, facilitation is nothing like teaching. We are all one in a group with a shared understanding, everyone takes a turn and there's no standing at the front. There is a pre-brief and a de-brief for each session and the questions and structure followed are led by the facilitators but they also join in each discussion and contribute continuously to the session. The similarities between teaching and facilitating were clear to me and I was amazed that someone could see those abilities and the potential in me to work in this way again. My occupational health review, when I left my teaching career behind, said I was "unfit to teach". I like to think what they meant was "too ill to teach" as the connotations of "unfit" still reverberate now.

The next time I went to a peer support workshop, the same facilitator who had asked me about training was again leading the course and I asked a few more questions about what was involved. I eventually signed up, completed my facilitator training a few years later and went on to volunteer for Leeds Mind for six years as a Group Work Facilitator. I then had an opportunity to join the Leeds Mind Peer Support Team for 18 months covering sickness absence. My new role was in the Community Mental Health Team (CMHT) working 1:1 with people by phone or over Zoom and supporting people by sharing all the things I found that helped me keep my bipolar disorder as stable as it's been for the past nine years. As part of this work, I shared a lot of the things that I've learned from the workshops and courses I've attended and facilitated for Leeds Mind as well as so much more from my recovery journey.

One thing I've learned, that has been a key factor in finding things that work for me, is to be open-minded. I didn't have a clue what would work for me and I felt that if I didn't try everything, I could potentially ignore that one technique that would revolutionise my life.

It's important to practise new skills when you're feeling okay; in other words, using meditation for the first time during a panic attack is rarely going to help. Practise and learn how to do it first. Perseverance has been essential for me. I didn't know what worked and helped until I had tried strategies repeatedly. If I found something that was really unhelpful or even triggering, this was useful knowledge and I refused to waste time on it but knowing it wasn't valuable was just as helpful as knowing things that were.

Sometimes, I have the opportunity to support people who are doing well and then the focus turns to what is working.

Why are they keeping well?

What do they need to look for as early warning signs of becoming unbalanced?

How do they maintain the status quo so that they stay well?

One of the first things I share with the people I support is the STRENGTH acronym that I shared in "The Early Days". What elements do you need in your life for you to function optimally? If all or most of these are being fulfilled, things are likely to be okay. Knowing what these are and being able to recognise subtle or even obvious changes can allow you to step in early. The earlier you notice triggers and/or changes in behaviour in your daily patterns, the easier it will be to get back on track.

The Wellbeing Flower

I also absolutely love this handout “The Wellbeing Flower” or WRAP (Wellness Recovery Action Plan). Firstly, it’s a cute flower and it’s visual. I’m a visual learner so anything I can visualise helps me to remember. The centre of the flower can be altered for lots of different scenarios: work, family occasions, anxiety, etc. Then you build the rest of the flower while thinking about what is required for you to keep well or to cope with the pressures associated with that particular scenario.

This plan has been designed so that you can be prepared for difficulties, both expected and unexpected. Recognising when your well-being may be in the early stages of decline allows you to intervene and put strategies in place to prevent you from ending up in a state of mental illness or distress.

- The **clouds** represent early warning signs that things are beginning to break down.
- The **umbrella** is the (WRAP) that protects the flower from the cloud.
- Each **petal** is a different self-care strategy. These are the wellness tools, anything that helps you cope or improves your mood either in the short term or the long term. For example, in the short term, you may go for a walk and spend some time in the fresh air and nature whilst a long-term plan might be to plan a trip away or an activity you enjoy like visiting the theatre.
- The **stalk** and **leaves** are the daily maintenance; the important things you do to look after yourself daily. These will include medication, self-care, nutrition, exercise and sleep. For the flower to be supported, a plant needs a strong stalk.

- The **watering can** represents your supporters; anyone you regard as part of your support network including friends, family, support workers, professionals and online forums.
- The **greenflies** are the triggers. Everyone's triggers are different and these can cause you to become unwell very quickly.
- The **insect spray** is your crisis plan. If you are unable to step in and change things and you become unwell, it's important to have a crisis plan. This may include having a place you can go to feel safe, professional support, phone numbers to call or text for immediate support such as the Samaritans, a friend or a particular coping strategy that you know helps.

The Wellbeing Flower was created by Sue Bird using the Wellness Recovery Action Plan that was developed by Mary Ellen Copeland.

The Stress Bucket

I also love the concept of the **stress bucket**. Imagine a bucket half full of water. Everything stressful in your life will be added to the bucket, for example, anxiety, work, a difficult conversation with a friend, bereavement, etc. To prevent the bucket from overflowing or your stress getting out of control and overwhelming, causing an inability to cope, the water/stress must be released somehow. This can be done in two ways; by reducing the stress into the bucket in the first place and by releasing the stress through the bottom of the bucket.

Imagine holes in the bottom of the bucket that allow the water to be drained. Each hole represents a strategy or technique you find useful to de-stress.

My holes are as follows: walking the dogs, chatting to my mum on the phone, meditation, Reiki, journaling, reading, watching something on TV, having a milky drink and many more. Some of these activities create a big hole in my bucket; a long walk in a beautiful place with my dogs can de-stress me for days whereas a milky drink might just help for an hour. Choosing different strategies depending on the time available and the impact required becomes easier with practice and, sometimes, I find myself reaching for just the right thing without conscious thought because I've done it so often.

Creating a stress bucket for yourself may take time. I always have a few of my holes empty as I know I'm open to trying new things and finding delight and calmness in unexpected places.

The Stress Bucket model was developed by Professor Alison Brabban and Dr Douglas Turkington.

The Poisonous Parrot

The Poisonous Parrot is another useful technique that I like to share. Again, this is very visual and I think that's one of the reasons I find it so useful.

We all have times in our lives when we hear a negative internal dialogue; that voice in your head that criticises you, belittles you or tells you that you're wrong. Imagine that voice isn't coming from in your head but instead is from a parrot sitting on your shoulder. We've all seen parrots on TV or at the zoo. They squawk a lot! If they are clever enough to talk, they do it in parrot fashion, they are repetitive and often don't make sense. They just repeat the same thing over and over and they can't have a proper conversation with you. This parrot is your inner critic. It doesn't have any evidence to back up what it says and, most of the time, it's just talking nonsense. Let's be honest, parrots are not very clever!

On your other shoulder is a beautiful wise owl. It's gentle and much quieter than the parrot so you may have to listen more carefully and tune in to its call. Because the owl is wise, it has a deeper insight into what is happening and speaks with compassion and kindness. The owl has a different perspective than the parrot and will give you hard facts that prove the parrot is a bit daft and doesn't know what it's talking about.

For example, you've slept in because the alarm didn't go off. The parrot immediately says you are stupid and a complete idiot for sleeping in and you will get in trouble at work for being late. The owl, on the other hand, has more sensible advice and points out that there was a power cut during the night causing your clock to reset and preventing your alarm from going off at the correct time. The owl advises that, if you remain focused, ignore social media and grab a banana to eat for breakfast on the way to work, you will save precious minutes and won't be as late as you first thought. The owl also reminds you that when you were late last year no one mentioned it. If you listen to the poisonous parrot and go into panic mode, you are less likely to stay focused on getting ready as quickly as you can, adrenaline and stress levels will soar and, before you know it, you will be even later and it will have an impact on most of your day.

By listening to the wise owl, you go into managing mode and everything isn't as bad as you first thought. To listen to your owl, you must first recognise your parrot. When it starts squawking, all you need to do initially is think, "Oh, my parrot is squawking". Once you get used to doing that, you can start to ask, "What's my owl saying?". Remember, it's quieter and you may need to listen more intently. If you aren't sure what the owl is saying, just identify the opposite of what the parrot saying, for example, if the parrot is saying, "You're stupid" then the owl is saying, "You're clever". It takes some practice because, at first, you may not believe your owl, mainly because you have been listening to your parrot for so long but, in time, the owl will become louder and you will hear it more easily.

Making Changes

When we want to make changes in our lives, it can feel daunting at first. In my peer support work, I've often encountered people who have a goal that they want to achieve and this is absolutely fantastic. The problem is that these goals are often really big things that, when looked at closely, require many steps to achieve them.

For example, what if someone wanted to go swimming? That sounds simple enough, doesn't it? So, let's add in the fact that this person doesn't live near a swimming pool that's accessible to them because they have a physical disability, chronic pain, limited finances and anxiety. Now it's a mountain to climb! Just like climbing a mountain, it's exhausting. It is achievable though, but it might take time and additional support to make it happen.

First, chop up the journey required to get to the pool into smaller steps. If the walk to the bus stop takes up all your energy right now, then short walks that build up to longer walks might be one of the first steps. You may have used SMART targets at work or school. SMART stands for specific, measurable, achievable, relevant and time-bound. So, set a target. It could be, "I will walk to the bus stop on Monday, Wednesday and Friday for two weeks". If this is too much once you've tried it, create a new SMART target with a shorter walk or fewer repetitions.

It's always important to be your own cheerleader when you are living with mental health issues. Don't beat yourself up if you only manage to do the walk twice but do celebrate those two walks you did manage. You will get there; be gentle with yourself as you've been unwell and taking on new challenges is tough. Bring your wise owl in to remind you how well you are doing.

CATS

Another similar strategy to use when you want to change things in your life is CATS which stands for consider, aims and take steps.

Consider – what do I find difficult? If I can increase my self-awareness around why some tasks are harder than others, I will be able to respond better to the things I want to change. First, I need to reflect on what changes are most difficult for me. Is it unexpected changes or things that take me out of my comfort zone? Belief - do I believe I can implement successful change in my life? Motivation - what is motivating me to want to implement change? Do I delay, distract or evade committing to making the changes?

Aims – are the goals that I am setting realistic and achievable? What do I need to put in place to aid my success? Goals - don't aim too high; make it a sensible and practical objective. Break it down into smaller more manageable steps that will allow me to gain confidence and increase my motivation to continue striving towards my goal. Practise - some things may need to be done numerous times to instil self-belief and motivation. I can also ask others for help, role-play or get support from a professional.

Take steps – to make change more manageable; it will be necessary to take smaller, easier steps first. Support - ask for help if needed and recognise the need for a support network. Self-care - when I am changing things in my life, I may get out of the habit of self-care so it's important to make time for this. Reward - plan rewards and celebrate my smaller successes along the way as I strive towards my final goal.

Source unknown

The Wellbeing Flower, Stress Bucket, Poisonous Parrot and CATS are just a few of the many strategies I've learned during my time volunteering at Leeds Mind. There are lots of resources on the national Mind website www.mind.org.uk and through many charities across the UK that support people with their mental health.

I can't fully express the value and progress I've been able to make as a result of peer support. I most definitely couldn't have gotten this far, learned so much about myself and my condition and remained so stable for such a long time without it.

As I said earlier in this chapter, it's magical!

I am a strong confident person

Just as it is!

Low Mood

So, it's not all sunshine and roses! Right now, I'm struggling with a depressive episode so, to keep it real and own my truth, here's what's happening in my life right now.

I'm really not sure what's causing this low mood, most probably a combination of things; living with constant pain after breaking my leg in four places several years ago, coming out of a global pandemic, winter and general family stuff. If you can work out the triggers of your depressive or hypomanic/manic episodes, it can be really helpful to identify areas of your life that need a bit more focus or it might just give you knowledge for the future about things to avoid. If they are unavoidable, you might need to consider putting in some extra strategies and self-care around these life events or challenges. I call this "a buffer." Sometimes, it's not obvious or I just don't know and that's okay too.

Even after all these years, I don't always notice the really early warning signs that something is not quite right but, once a few of these things are happening simultaneously, it becomes more apparent. There are also times when family and friends notice things aren't quite right before I do. For me, this is a vital part of my ability to accept all is not well so, if someone points something out to me, I need to respect their perspective and I know historically they are usually right. It's like a tangled ball of wool. It's hard to unravel what's happening but my first symptoms tend to be fatigue, the kind of tiredness a good night's sleep doesn't fix, and lack of motivation to do the things which I only notice when things have fallen out of my routine such as regular cacao, long walks with the dogs and preparing healthy meals. There's an increased use of scrolling on social media and playing games on my iPad. Brain fog is definitely worse; I make mistakes and am more forgetful. I have realised that I've stopped making lists and using planning grids so it's no wonder I'm forgetting things. As it gets worse, my hygiene routine and my medication are also being affected.

On the flip side, I have days when I have energy to spare and I can be really active and productive but this results in sheer exhaustion the following day. At this point, I know an increase in medication is going to be on the table but, for now, I'm opting to stick to my current dosage, investing time in self-care and making the balance between rest and activity more even. So, that's where I'm at but what am I doing about it?

Luckily, the spring weather is making an appearance, with the lighter nights and some sunshine enabling me to get out for longer walks with the dogs and I counterbalance this with a rest in the afternoon. This rest is time-limited. I'm treating myself to a milky coffee and I've started reading again; there's nothing like lying on my bed or the sofa with a bit of gritty crime fiction; pure escapism from my world. There have been a few bubble baths, self-massage and listening to podcasts and audiobooks and I've been setting a few rules for myself such as taking my meds on time every time, not missing any, and sticking to the menu plan so I keep eating healthily.

Mornings have been a total nightmare. I just don't want to get out of bed and, despite the alarm being set, I press the snooze button. Mornings just feel overwhelming as I have a lot to do first thing every day.

Support is vital, as is talking about my feelings as I ruminate less if everything is out in the open. I'm really lucky that I have a supportive family and I'm able to ask for help. So, now my husband is also setting his alarm for the morning and he's feeding the dogs. These two really minor changes have made an enormous impact and I've also started to do tasks the evening before, just to reduce that feeling of overwhelm the following morning.

I talk to my family about going "back to basics" and, even after using this phrase for years, I always get the same response "What do you mean?" What I mean is stripping things back, making sure my diary isn't too full but also planning time with friends as that's a good way for me to recharge my batteries; avoiding isolation, lists and planning; tackling one thing at a time; healthy food, meds, good hydration, gentle exercise, time outside in the fresh air and rest; and including things in my day such as meditation, giving myself Reiki, drinking cacao and journalling as these things have served me well in the past.

So, it's been a week since I wrote the previous paragraphs and, by investing time in self-care, breathing and focusing my attention, I've really turned a corner. I got paper, a pen and a cup of coffee and then sat down and planned my week. I use a weekly planning sheet and put all the work things in first, then the hobby stuff and time with friends, meals are planned around how much time I have each evening to cook and housework can be put in too.

It's not completely fixed and things can obviously be moved about but it helps remove my feelings of overwhelm. The weather has definitely helped; I had a two-hour dog walk down by the river where it's safe to let them off their leads and I listened to an audiobook. I made sure my meds were taken on time.

An affirmation has just popped up on my phone saying, "I will invest in myself because I am worth it." Very fitting and true. I've chosen to invest more time in myself over these past few weeks, not only because I am worth it but also because I don't want to feel so rubbish and other people and my dogs are reliant on me.

I also attended a Radiant Woman's Circle; the spirit dance element of the session opened the floodgates and the tears flowed down my cheeks. I'm pretty good at holding back tears but I think there's a real benefit in releasing tension in this way and, afterwards, I noticed a real shift. I decided to pull an Oracle card each morning, get back to drinking cacao and try to journal a bit more. So now, I put down my iPad in the evening and use my time more wisely. I will admit that I'm doing better with these things but I haven't managed to do them every day and that's okay as putting myself under pressure would be counterproductive. Just be gentle and kind to yourself when things are tough; they won't last forever and small changes can make a big impact on your mood.

Reiki

If you're reading this book, you probably fall into one of three camps when it comes to Reiki: either you've never heard of it, you've heard of it but don't know much about it or you know exactly what it is and its numerous benefits.

Reiki is a hands-on, non-invasive complementary therapy originating in Japan. The word "Reiki" comes from the combination of the Japanese words Rei (which means universal life) and Ki (which means energy). In Reiki, we refer to Universal Lifeforce Energy which is energy that is all around us, on earth, in space and all living things and inanimate objects. In other cultures, this may be referred to by other names but it's the same regardless of what you call it.

Reiki is a method of natural healing. The Reiki practitioner is a channel through which the healing energy flows into the person they are treating where it is used for their highest good. Reiki cannot harm. It can be used to alleviate the symptoms of both physical and mental illness or can be used to aid relaxation. It is a holistic system for balancing, healing and bringing harmony to all aspects of a person.

I'm including some information about the origins and history of Reiki as I think it's really interesting. Reiki is a relatively new complementary therapy and anyone who is initiated into Usui Reiki can trace their lineage back to Mikao Usui, the founder of the most commonly used branch of Reiki. I can trace my lineage back to Mr. Usui in 6 steps.

The History of Reiki

Mikao Usui

Mikao Usui was born in 1865. It is believed that Mikao Usui developed the practice of Reiki in the 1920s. He was brought up as a Tendai Buddhist and, as a child, he entered a Tendai Buddhist monastery near Mount Kurama. Here, he studied martial arts, spiritual teachings and working with energies. He had a keen interest in psychology, medicine, including both traditional Chinese medicine and Western medicine, and the theology of different religions. He studied a great deal and also began Zen Buddhist training in 1922 and many of the things he learned may have contributed to the system he developed.

Usui studied to try and discover what the purpose of life was after enlightenment he said it was “Anshin Rytsu Mei” - your mind being at peace, knowing what to do with your life and not being bothered by anything. In other words, a search for peace and contentment. It was at this point that he went to Mount Kurama for a 21-day meditation and fast. It was during this time that he had a spiritual awakening and developed the self-healing system we know today as Reiki.

When Mr Usui returned from the mountains, he opened a Reiki clinic and began to teach the practice. His teaching was broken down into three levels: Level 1/Shoden, Level 2/Okuden and Master Level/Shinpiden. He taught over 2,000 students but only 20 of them were approved to teach. One of these people was Chujiro Hayashi. Mr. Usui asked Hayashi to open a Reiki clinic, which he did, and so the learning was spread further as more students were attuned to Reiki. Mr. Usui passed away in 1926.

Chujiro Hayashi

Hayashi studied with Usui and gained his Master Level in 1925 when he was 47. He was a naval physician who combined his medical training and Reiki knowledge. He kept detailed notes of the treatments he provided and created "standard" hand positions to be used during treatments. This was different to Usui's approach which was simpler and more intuitive. One of the people who came to his clinic for treatment was Hawayo Takata. She had travelled from her home in Hawaii and was so amazed by the results of the Reiki in treating the various ailments she had that she asked Hayashi to teach her Reiki. He agreed as he was keen to attune another woman in Reiki as, at that point in time, he had taught only his wife.

Hawayo Takata

In 1937, Hayashi travelled to Hawaii where he stayed for several months with Hawayo Takata. Hawaiian-born Takata had a hard life. She was widowed at the age of 34 and was left to raise her two young children alone. She worked incredibly hard and it took its toll on her health. She was suffering from stomach pain, a lung condition and mental health issues. Following the death of her sister, she travelled to Japan to break the news to her parents. Whilst in Japan, she was admitted to hospital and told she needed an operation. Instead, she visited Hayashi's Reiki clinic. It was not a technique she was familiar with but, once she began receiving treatments, her symptoms began to improve and, within four months, she was healed. She wanted to learn Reiki for herself. Once she had reached Level 2, she returned to Hawaii along with Hayashi. She was initiated as a Reiki Master and set up several Reiki clinics. Reiki had been introduced to the Western world! Takata travelled to the USA mainland to treat clients and was known to give lengthy treatments and to treat people daily over many months. She would also attune family members so they could also give Reiki to her client. Takata thought the Japanese system of Reiki would be too complicated for Westerners to understand so she simplified the system to only eight hand positions. Without Takata, it's most likely that Reiki would have become an obscure practice known only to a few people.

The Spirituality of Reiki

There's evidence of energy healing for thousands of years across different cultures and religions. The Japanese call it Ki, the Chinese call it Chi, Christians refer to it as the Holy Spirit and Hindus call it Prana. Reiki is not a religion but it does promote living a life of harmony, treating others with compassion and committing yourself to be peaceful and to promote peace to those around you. Your intentions should be pure, genuine and honest as these are universal attributes across all cultures. Mr. Usui created the Five Principles of Reiki.

"The secret art of inviting happiness

The miraculous medicine of all diseases

Just for today, do not anger

Do not worry and be filled with gratitude

Devote yourself to your work

Be kind to people

Every morning and evening, join your hands in prayer

Pray these words to your heart

and chant these words with your mouth."

USUI REIKI TREATMENT FOR THE IMPROVEMENT OF BODY AND MIND

THE FOUNDER

USUI MIKAO

Reiki Principles

For today only:
Do not anger
Do not worry
Be humble
Be honest in your work
Be compassionate to yourself
and others

Reiki Principles in Japanese

Kyoh dake wa
Ikaru - na
Shinpai suna
Kansha shite
Gyo wo hage me
Hito ni shinsetsu ni

PRONUNCIATION:
KYOH DAKE WA – KYOH – DAKEH – WAY
IKARU – NA – IKARU – NAH
SHINPAI SUNA – SHIN-PIE SUE-NAH
KANSHA SHITE – KANSHA SH-TEH
GYO WO HAGE ME – GO-O HAGEH – MEH
HITO NI SHINSETSU NI – HEETO NEE SHIN-SET-TZU NEE

You can chant the principles in English or Japanese as a mantra or prayer. This, alongside self-Reiki, is encouraged as a daily practice.

The teachings of Reiki are sacred and I was always taught to keep many things to myself. If you choose to learn Reiki, those sacred teachings will unfold to you piece by piece as they should. It's an awakening and amazing journey.

Reiki Treatments

So, what happens when you go for a Reiki treatment? The Reiki practitioner will start by taking a brief medical history. Your treatment will take place with you either sitting in a chair or lying on a massage bed. You remain fully clothed for the treatment which will last either 30 minutes or 60 minutes. The Reiki practitioner will place their hands on your body or hold them just above you if you prefer not to be touched. They will move their hands to different positions on/over your body. You may hear the practitioner breathing deeply as they draw energy into their body. Soothing music will be played and candles may be lit. Where the practitioner has placed their hands, you may feel changes in temperature either hot or cold. You may experience a tingling sensation. You may feel a deep sense of relaxation and calm. You may not feel anything at all. Sometimes, people fall asleep during a treatment.

The sensations you feel, or the lack of sensation, is not an indicator of Reiki; it's purely your body's way of sensing the energy. When the practitioner has finished, they will gently touch you on the shoulder or speak to you and you will be given time to relax and sit up when you are ready. The Reiki healing continues long after the treatment has finished.

Uses of Reiki

- For all living things: humans, animals and plants;
- For physical and mental health;
- As a complimentary therapy alongside traditional medicine;
- For events/trauma in the past and the future;
- To find lost things;
- For use in hospices, hospital settings and animal sanctuaries.

Distance Reiki

Think back to your physics lessons at school. You will have been taught the concept that energy can never be destroyed. It can be transformed from one type of energy to another but it's everlasting. This is an essential concept and understanding needed to comprehend how distance Reiki healing works.

In the past, before we had the internet, Wi-Fi or mobile phones, we would have had a hard time imagining that we would be able to send a photo to someone in a text message on the other side of the world and that they would be able to receive it within seconds. We would have found it hard to believe that this kind of technology and transmission could exist. Think about radio waves, microwaves and X-rays. You can't see them, but you can hear or see their effects.

Well, Reiki works in just the same way. I've sent Reiki to people and animals across the world and they have felt the same effects as if I had laid my hands on them in person. It's quite amazing to have an energetic connection with someone you've never met and to provide healing and comfort. I will be honest, it took me a while to get my head around it but, once I thought of it in terms of science and I heard the difference it was making to others and the way I felt when people sent Reiki to me from afar, I was blown away by this.

My Reiki Journey

My Reiki journey began whilst I was being supported by the Richmond Fellowship charity which helps people with mental health problems to find or stay in work. Also, attending appointments and courses gave me something to get up for each day and encouraged me to push myself to get out of the house and socialise. I was also beginning to realise the benefits of surrounding myself with others who were dealing with mental health issues, the people who "got it" and who could share the things they were finding that helped. So when I was invited to take part in a confidence-building course I said 'Yes, sign me up,'

Chris Krow Summers was the course facilitator and I really enjoyed the sessions, Chris' teaching style and exploring different aspects of confidence building. During the last session, Chris asked me if I would be interested in joining his sessions to learn Reiki. I'm so grateful that I was open-minded to the new opportunities presented to me while in the early stages of recovery. I would definitely not be as stable as I am now had I not been willing to engage in different things with a wide range of people who were able to share so much knowledge that I didn't even know I didn't know.

My first Reiki session began with an attunement, a sacred ritual shared by my Reiki Master, Chris and myself along with the rest of the group. The attunement facilitates the Reiki Master's connection with the Universal Life Force Energy to help open the heart and intuition of the student. This was such a beautiful experience. Even before Chris placed his hands on my head, I could feel a surge of energy around me and I could tell he was near despite having my eyes closed. I felt warm and could see the changes of the light through the window, a warm golden glow on my eyelids, but when I opened my eyes the sky outside was cloudy. Every time I've experienced an attunement or reju (when the Reiki Master draws as much Ki into a student as part of an energetic clearing), I've experienced a heightened sense of smell. All the scents in the room become magnified like each individual scent is right under my nose. Following this first attunement, there was a sudden shift in my abilities and I was able to feel energy in a totally new way. Over many weeks, the group members practised giving Reiki to each other alongside in-depth teachings. I would urge you to be cautious about engaging with the wide variety of courses that claim to attune students over the internet or teach you everything in a day. Beware! Nothing can compare to the teachings and repetition of an extended course in a group setting. You learn through practice, sharing and guidance.

Self-Reiki is the focus of Reiki Level 1 or Shoden level. It's very difficult to heal someone else if you are not compassionate enough to turn that healing firstly on yourself, to embark on a journey of self-improvement and self-care. It was through this process that I began to make new friends who were travelling spiritual journeys and awakenings and who introduced me to a range of new opportunities and shared new knowledge and information with me. I've always loved learning new things so I was like a sponge soaking up everything around me and exploring new possibilities. I've completed my Level 1, Level 2 and Level 2 Advanced Reiki so far. Reiki Master and Teacher level will present itself when I'm ready but, for now, I have enough skills to be going on with.

I planned on opening a Reiki business but Covid stopped that when the first lockdown came into place just weeks after I had launched my business. I started working for Leeds Mind and so I'm helping people through peer support. I receive excellent feedback from the people I support and, through that and an epiphany when I was doing womb healing work (more about this later), I realised that I needed to share my knowledge on a wider platform to help people manage their mental health. And so, the idea for this book was born. Everything appears just when it should in divine timing so, whilst I'm writing and supporting people to manage their own mental health, I continue to do Reiki at no charge to the client and one day the stars will align and my Reiki business will relaunch.

October 2023

As I knew it would, the opportunity to extend my Reiki training and complete my Reiki Master and Reiki Teacher levels presented itself. Often, the training had been on a weekend when I work but, for the first time, Chris was offering the training over four sessions in the evening.

You may think that becoming a Reiki Master is the end of the journey but it's definitely the beginning. Sacred teachings were shared in the sessions and I had the chance to meet with a new group of students and embark on another voyage of discovery and strengthen my love of Reiki.

For me, it has been a privilege and an honour not only to have learned Reiki but also to be able to use it to help myself and others. It's a key tool in my mental health toolbox. My understanding and ability to heal myself through Reiki have been the greatest catalyst in my recovery journey. I've learned a skill that's incredibly powerful, free, simple and easy to use anywhere and anytime.

I find it helps me to manage my anxiety levels especially when travelling. I've stopped a migraine in its tracks, reduced my pain levels when recovering from breaking my leg in four places and I also use it for a bit of relaxing "me time". I also had the honour of giving Reiki to my Gran in her final days of life at a moment when I had nothing else to give. I felt useful and able to support her in a way only I knew at that time. I've sent Reiki to 97 Westies every hour on the hour for days around bonfire night. I offered this through a Facebook Westie group, slideshows of dogs and a cat on my iPad to channel my healing energy to dogs all over the world. I've more recently sent Reiki to a gorgeous lamb born with a disability. I reached out to the animal sanctuary who were so grateful and I sent Reiki every day for a week until the sad news came that he hadn't made it. But I made a difference through the energetic connection with owners and animals and the thankfulness received that someone was offering to help. An act of kindness and love.

Reiki conference

During lockdown, I attended the UK Reiki Federation online conference. The highlight for me was listening to the current Reiki lineage holder, Johannes Reindl. I was in awe learning about his Reiki journey. I expected to hear something profound and amazing but his message was simple; practise self-Reiki every day. I will admit, I fall short of this despite a nightly reminder on my phone. It's something I should really challenge myself to as I have a feeling it would be completely transformative. Out of everything, I've learned that if I could only keep one thing to manage my mental health and anxiety and to make an impact on my physical health, it would be Reiki.

Emotional Freedom Technique

I first learned about the Emotional Freedom Technique (EFT), also known as Tapping, as part of my wider Reiki training as it's another form of energy healing. I will be totally honest with you; it's not something I use but, over the years, as a peer support worker I've shared it with many people and some have even described it as a "game changer" and have begun using it as a daily practice so I felt it was important that I share it with you.

EFT involves tapping certain points of your face, head and upper body. These points are called meridian points or acupressure points. Energy moves around your body along specific channels. You can tap into this energy anywhere along the system. When you feel a negative emotion, it can have a mental and physical effect on your body and your body's energy is disrupted. Tapping can restore your energy balance.

Tapping reduces stress. When you feel fear, worry, anxiety or other negative emotions, this triggers a response in a part of your brain called the amygdala, often referred to as the "fight or flight response." When you are stressed, the levels of the hormone cortisol (often called the stress hormone) rise in your body. This is a great way to protect you from real danger but often our amygdala reacts to things that aren't an immediate threat. So, I've gone all scientific on you but there's more science about what is happening in your brain when you tap! Tapping sends a calming message to your brain and your body then responds by relaxing. EFT regulates your nervous system and this, in turn, boosts the immune system and your body is returned to the parasympathetic (relaxation) nervous system response. Cortisol levels in the bloodstream are reduced. If you want even more science, just google "EFT scientific studies" as there's a lot of information out there. Very fascinating!

It's estimated that 10 million people worldwide have used tapping! Wow! Whilst researching this for the book, I've wondered why I'm not using this technique more, especially when I'm struggling with my travel anxiety. It's a fascinating technique being used widely in schools and with children. It's simple and extremely effective. It must be empowering for youngsters to be able to manage their emotions whilst being given a vocabulary to express how they feel. I also discovered that it's being used in places of natural and human-made disasters. This is quite an old quote but it shows the scale around the world to which it's being utilised.

~

"Energy psychology has been applied in the wake of natural and human-made disasters in the Congo, Guatemala, Indonesia, Kenya, Kosovo, Kuwait, Mexico, Moldova, Nairobi, Rwanda, South Africa, Tanzania, Thailand and the US. At least three international humanitarian relief organisations have adapted energy psychology as a treatment in their post-disaster missions."

David Feinstein PhD, Journal of Traumatology March 2008.

~

So don't take my word for it that EFT is fabulous, have a go. It's quick and simple. I've included some photographs to help you tap at the correct places. Here is a step-by-step guide on how to tap.

The Technique

1. Find a quiet place to sit. What emotion are you struggling with right now? For this step-by-step guide, I am going to use the emotion of anxiety.

2. Give your current level of anxiety a number from 0 to 10 depending on how severe it is, where 0 is the least anxious and 10 is the most.

3. Create a sentence that you will repeat with each different part of your body you will tap on. You may choose one of the following; "Even though I am anxious, I completely and deeply love myself", "Even though I feel this anxiety, I accept how I feel", "Even though I am anxious, I give my body permission to relax".

4. Use your first and middle fingers to tap. You will tap with your dominant hand.

5. Your first tapping point is on the side of your hand.

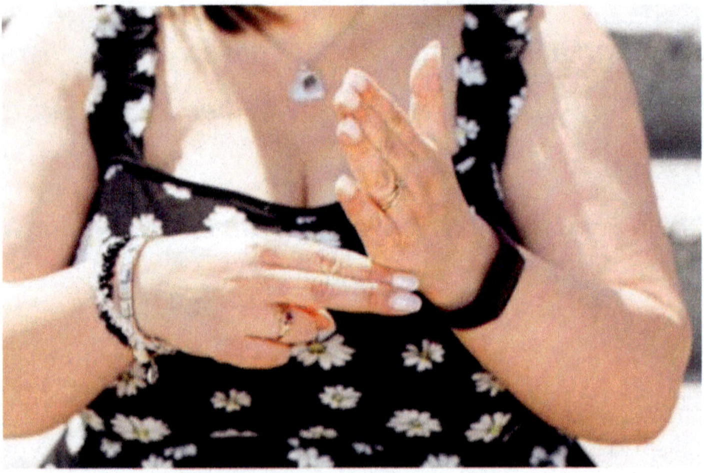

6. As you tap say the sentence you have created aloud.

7. Next tap on the crown of your head, again saying the sentence aloud.

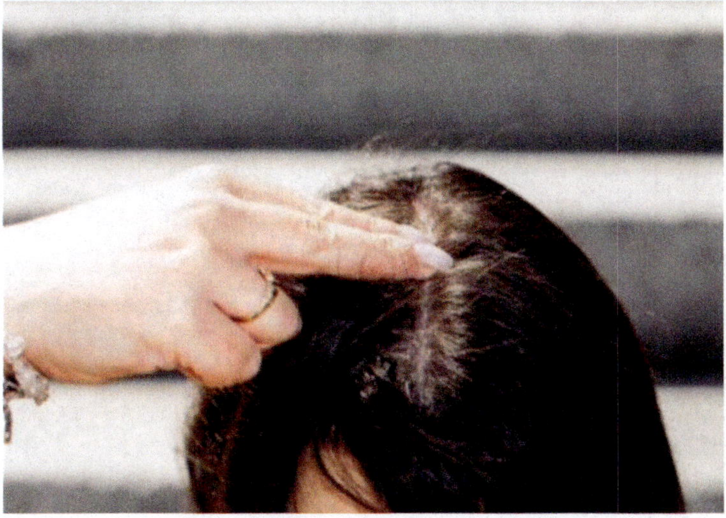

8. Continue this as you tap:

- above your eyebrow;

- at the side of your eye;

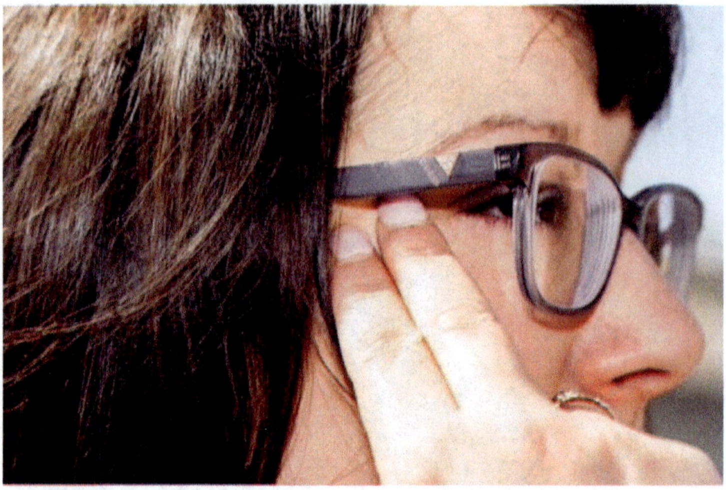

- under your eye;

- under your nose on your philtrum;

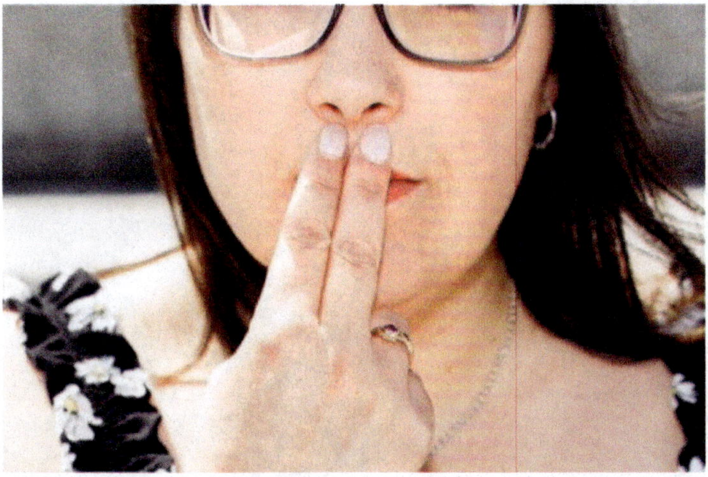

- on your chin;

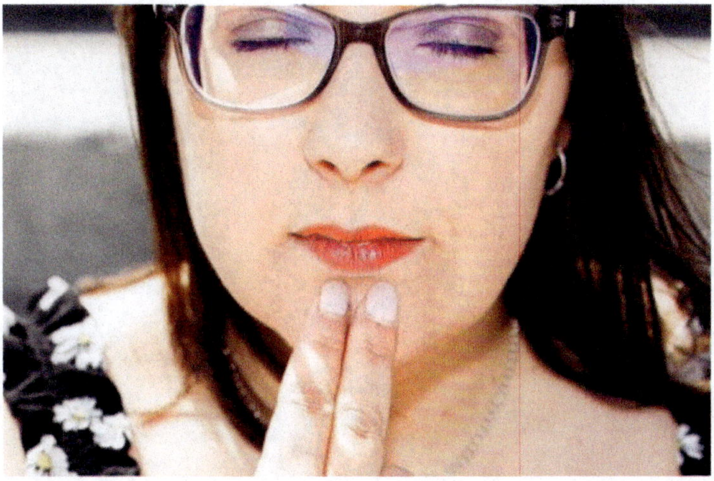

- on your collarbone;

- and finally, under your arm.

9. Now mark your anxiety/emotion level from 0 – 10 again. Has it gone down? It may have gone down enough that one cycle of EFT is enough in this case. If not, repeat the tapping cycle again and again until the level of your emotion is manageable. This may be 0 or a low number.

You can use EFT for a whole range of emotions and as often as you feel it necessary during the day.

For more information, check out www.thetappingsolution.com and their YouTube channel for excellent videos to guide you.

I am on a journey of growth and self discovery

Just as it is!

When things don't turn out as planned

So, it's Easter weekend, my mood is significantly more stable and life is good. My self-care practices have increased and the weather is better too, which definitely makes an impact.

But what happens when the plans you have made suddenly get tipped upside down? The dream weekend - unexpected time off work as the lady I support is in respite for the weekend. I'm going to enjoy walking the dogs and tiring them out. Then I'll go to my favourite local tea shop, Rivers Meet, find a quiet table in the corner and sit writing this book. I will set up a tab and keep the coffee flowing, have a bite of lunch and a lovely slice of homemade cake. I used to do this when I was writing my dissertation. I was much more productive there than if I had sat at home as there was always a distraction or a washing machine that needed emptying. What has actually happened is that my husband has tested positive for Covid and I've locked him in the attic until he is better! No really, our bedroom is in the eaves of our house and has an ensuite so he's fine up there. I'm sleeping on the sofa and we are communicating by text. So far, this is working really well and the fact I'm writing this means I haven't totally dismissed the plan although the motivation to write anything other than this "Just as it is" piece has proven elusive.

I've prepared all the vegetables and I'm cooking beef and lamb joints today ready for Easter Sunday dinner as the plan was that my husband would be cooking it. I've poured myself a glass of alcohol-free wine; this is a relatively new find for me and it actually tastes like wine, unlike grape juice in a glass bottle pretending to be wine.

I sat down at the table and was instantly distracted by Facebook. To be fair, I was posting a question in an advice group because Fudge is having trouble with his anal glands (told you I would write about things exactly as they are) so it didn't feel like a waste of time.

I do know that I won't make much writing progress today. I'm really tired and don't feel like I can do justice to the book today. And that's okay; sometimes we have to just accept that the best-made plans don't come to fruition and that tomorrow is another day. Don't get me wrong, I'm disappointed that my four days off work and the plans I've made have had to change course but I know from experience that sometimes these things happen for a reason and everything turns out fine. I need to be here in the house because I need to look after my husband, making him plenty of drinks and wholesome food, all delivered to the bedroom door. Fudge also needs looking after and I have to put calendula compresses on his sore bottom.

The sun is shining; it's Easter so there's plenty of chocolate around; the joint of beef in the oven smells delicious and tomorrow is another day to work on this book. Got to go! Fudge has just been sick in the garden and if I don't get there quickly Foggy will eat it!

For more delightful stories about life with dogs, there's an entire chapter on "Dogs and Other Animals" and how they make a positive impact on our mental well-being.

Mindfulness & Meditation

Mindfulness

Mindfulness is NOT Meditation

I feel that there are a lot of misconceptions about mindfulness. We see and hear the word everywhere now, in conversation, on social media and on TV.

So, here's what I think it is: mindfulness is a state of mind where you are 100% focused and in the zone and where you are not distracted by your thoughts or the events unfolding around you.

Meditation is a form of mindfulness that can be an excellent strategy to help you relax and manage your anxiety levels. I will delve further into meditation later in this chapter but, for now, back to mindfulness.

You will be in a state of mindfulness at various times throughout the day but it's likely that you won't be aware of it. Activities that promote a true state of mindfulness will differ from person to person. For me, listening to birdsong or enjoying the feel of the water cascading over me in the shower provides moments of mindful bliss. On the other hand, my brother finds his most mindful moments when he is downhill mountain biking with mud flicking up behind him as he gathers speed. That adrenaline-fueled escape is my worst nightmare but is his preferred form of escape from the stresses of daily life.

If you haven't used mindfulness techniques before, I would recommend starting small and building up. People I've spoken with who try to do a 20-minute guided meditation in times of extreme mental distress are highly likely to find it impossible to focus on listening to the words. Try to practise the techniques for the first time when you are calm and unlikely to be interrupted.

During my first experiences with mindfulness, I tried to 100% totally focus on the here and now as I was doing routine daily tasks such as brushing my teeth, peeling carrots or walking the dogs. Here's what I did:

Mindful teeth brushing

Look carefully at what you are doing. How does the top feel in your fingers as you remove it from the tube of toothpaste? Can you smell the toothpaste immediately? If not, have a sniff of the tube. Watch the toothpaste as it squeezes out of the tube and onto the toothbrush. Look at the different textures and the contrast between brush and toothpaste. Raise the toothbrush to your mouth. Does the brush feel different now that the paste is on it?

Take your time to brush your teeth, focusing on how the brush feels in your mouth and as it makes contact with each tooth. It may help to close your eyes or you can watch your progress in a mirror.

Continue to brush your teeth as you normally would but pay close attention to what you are doing, the physical sensations and the overall experience.

Using your senses

It's particularly useful to work through the list of your senses. What can you see? What can you hear, touch, smell and taste? Five senses, one minute per sense and, just like that, you've completed a five-minute mindfulness exercise. Your mind will wander as that's what minds do but the trick to mindfulness is not to stop your mind wandering but to notice when it has and bring it back to the task at hand, whatever that may be. When you do this, you are controlling your mind and thoughts.

You can apply the same practice as I've described to other daily tasks. You will quickly develop the skills of noticing your mind wandering and bringing it back to the here and now. Give yourself a pat on the back and celebrate your successes. Build up to practising mindfulness several times a day. Your confidence will improve and then you might decide to try it at a time when you are in emotional difficulty.

Don't get angry if you find it difficult, because it is difficult. Some days, our brains are busier than others and, some days, mindfulness will come easier than others. Be kind to yourself and, if it's really tough and you are struggling to focus right now, leave it and try again later.

The best thing about mindfulness is that you can do it any time anywhere and no one you will know. A few other ideas to try include:

Malteser melting moments - hold a Malteser or other small piece of food (raisin, sweet, chocolate). Use your senses. How does it feel in your hand? This sensation may change as the heat of your hand makes the Malteser melt. Use your other senses. Smell it, lick it, pop it in your mouth and hold it there. What does it feel like? How does it taste and smell? Is there a sound as it melts and dissolves? How does your tongue feel as you move it around your mouth?

Walking - focus particularly on your hearing for this exercise. What can you hear? The sound of your footsteps? Other people? I often have my dogs with me so I can hear the patter of paws, dog tags banging off collars and the odd bark. I can also hear the hum of the motorway from outside my house, birdsong and the leaves on the trees dancing in the breeze. If I listen really carefully, I can hear sounds from the grass.

On the bus - I spy! Not just a child's game. Just look around you.

Meditation

Now let's turn our attention to meditation which can take many different forms. You can practise meditation alone or with other people; you can attend a group, use an app, YouTube videos or simply focus on your own breath or the things around you. Your choice may be dictated by how much time you have or, after trying a few different ways of meditating, you may have a favourite or a particular method that you find easier. Whatever you choose to do, even if only for a few minutes, meditation can promote calmness and self-awareness. Breathwork or breathing techniques are an effective way to control or slow your breathing down, having a direct impact on your respiratory, cardiovascular and autonomic nervous system. It's so beneficial for promoting calmness, reducing anxiety and lowering blood pressure. My two favourite techniques are:

Counted breaths

Sit or lie comfortably with your eyes closed.

~~

Breathe in for a count of four

Pause

Breathe out for a count of five

Pause

Breathe in for a count of five

Pause

Breathe out for a count of six

Pause

Breathe in for a count of six

Pause

Breathe out for a count of seven

Pause

Breathe in for a count of seven.

Pause

Breathe out for a count of eight

Pause

Repeat the breathing in for seven and out for eight for five to ten minutes or however long you have available.

~~

I find that counting helps me to focus and my mind is less likely to wander.

Single Nostril Breathing

This is a type of yoga breathing which may be used as part of the relaxation method at the end of a yoga class which is where I learned it.

~~

Sit comfortably with your eyes closed.

~~

Close the right nostril by applying gentle pressure with your thumb

Place your middle and index fingers between your eyebrows

Inhale deeply through your left nostril

Exhale deeply through your left nostril

After exhaling release your right thumb from your right nostril

and

Close the left nostril by applying gentle pressure with your index finger

Inhale deeply through your right nostril

Exhale deeply through your right nostril

Now release your ring finger from your left nostril

Repeat by closing each nostril in turn

Inhaling and exhaling through the open nostril

~~

Repeat for a few minutes.

~~

Guided Meditation

Guided meditation is a type of meditation led by a teacher, either in person or via audio or video.

You might want to read the following guided meditation aloud and record it on your phone so you can close your eyes and fully relax as you picture the meditation like a movie playing in your head.

Before you start get into a comfortable position, either sitting or lying down. Make sure you won't be disturbed.

Your mind may well wonder. That's okay as it is what minds do. Just try to bring yourself back to listening to or reading the meditation. It doesn't matter how many times your mind wanders the important thing is that you notice and bring it back to the present moment. You may like to try writing your own meditation to take you to a place far away. It didn't take me long to write my own meditation as I simply focused on my different senses and what I could see, hear and feel.

Forest Meditation

You're walking along a dusty path and, in the distance, you see a forest. The sun feels warm on your face and there is a gentle breeze that causes your hair to move against your face.

As you approach the trees, you can see their leaves rustling slightly and you can hear them as they brush against each other. You hear birds, chirping and trilling as they call to each other, hidden from sight, high amongst the foliage of the trees.

The path enters the forest and immediately you notice the change in the light and temperature as you are engulfed by the shade. As you walk across the path, strewn with leaves and sticks crunching and crackling under your feet, you notice shadows on the forest floor. You walk on slowly, taking deep breaths, taking in all the scents of the forest.

As you move along the path, you are suddenly bathed in sunlight that shines through the canopy of the trees. It's cooler in the forest but the sunlight adds a sudden burst of heat on your face. You tip your head toward the sun and close your eyes, enjoying the sensation of the heat that moves across your skin with the breeze.

You stand for a while then continue to walk onwards along the path; you stretch your arms out wide and your fingertips brush against the leaves and branches. You pause to explore a leaf with your fingers; it's waxy to the touch and your thumb slides effortlessly across the smooth, shiny surface. You hold the leaf above you so the light cascades upon it and suddenly you can see the veins like rivers flowing, interconnecting with each other and creating a green tinge on your cheeks. You let go of the leaf and it spirals and falls effortlessly to the ground.

You continue through the forest, taking pauses every now and then to ensure you don't miss a thing. Then you hear a new sound; it's a babbling brook winding between the trees and, as you turn the corner, you see a waterfall crashing into the small lake the river flows into. You cup your hands together and scoop water from the waterfall, take an ice-cold sip that you can feel all the way down into your stomach as you swallow it. Next, you splash water onto your face; you feel your skin tighten and a sound escapes your mouth at the shock of the cold.

There is a moss-covered log beside the waterfall for you to sit on. You may sit here as long as you want, listening to the harmony of birds and the rush of the waterfall.

Enjoy this calmness; let feelings of peace wash over you. Whenever you are ready, you can turn back along the path, remembering that this walk has a completely different view of the forest than you saw as you entered.

When you depart the forest, take with you the calmness and tranquillity you received and let it be with you for the rest of your day.

Rest is
productive

Just As It Is!

Why me?

So, the book was complete and the editing process was well underway when it became clear that another *Just As It Is* section was required.

This morning, I had no idea what I was going to write about but then, like so much of this book, it became crystal clear. I came in from a long walk in the pouring rain with the dogs. We were drenched! I grabbed some towels and flicked them open to lay on the floor when, ping, something went in my lower back. Instant agony! The dogs dried themselves as best they could whilst I hobbled about.

Next, I came out in a hot sweat and alarms started beeping on my insulin pump. I stuffed Jelly Babies into my mouth but still my levels were going down - 4.4, 3.2, 2.8. I've just started using a new insulin pump that's supposed to be life-changing. It communicates with the blood sugar sensor and alters the insulin rate accordingly. Amazing! Except, it takes time to learn your patterns and obviously it hasn't learnt mine yet. On top of that, I'm using the activity setting that keeps your blood sugar at 8.6. Well, that hasn't worked! Worst hypoglycaemia I've had in years!

So, today, I'm having a "Why me?" day! Why am I lumbered with chronic pain after breaking my leg; back pain; tennis elbow for the past 6 months; Type 1 Diabetes and bipolar in a post-manic phase? I'm managing self-care, painkillers and ibuprofen gel for my back; I have my yoga mat out for some gentle stretches; and I also left a pool of tears on my mat as I sobbed uncontrollably. I think sometimes you need a good cry. It's a release of a build-up of tension. Today just feels too much, like everything is stacked against me and life is too hard. The negative thoughts have started to invade my mind at this point. I must have done something terrible to deserve all this, I'm a horrible person and my family shouldn't be burdened with me, etc.

Luckily, I've experienced far worse than this in the past. In the past, this negative thinking has lasted for days or weeks. Now, I'm quicker to identify the negativity and I can step in and intercept thoughts. I had some tasks to do as we were getting ready to go to my mum's that afternoon. Being busy and focusing on something is a good strategy for me. I put Fia on to listen to as I was on the yoga mat and, as I finished packing, I moved gently to minimise the twinges in my back. I drank some cacao and set the intention of "every experience is an opportunity to learn". However, I'm not sure what today has taught me; maybe it's just that I have control over my thoughts. The negative thoughts will be there but I don't have to listen and engage. I can tackle them with truths. I am loved and cherished by many people. I'm stubborn and fiercely independent. I ask for help when I need it but I'm not a burden. My health is complicated but manageable, nothing life-limiting. All I need to do is look around me and I can see joy in the little things.

Today's been tough but it's only one day! In fact, it's only been one part of the day. I've typed this in the car whilst travelling to my mum's. Again, being focused has helped with my PTSD symptoms and very soon I will see my mum, stepdad, brother, sister-in-law and nephew. So, today is turning into a great day!

Finding My Tribe

Women's Circles and Oh My Goddess Retreat!

So, lockdown during the Covid pandemic was actually a real boost in terms of my spirituality. Not only was I more aware of the things in life that were important to me and that I was grateful for but also Zoom came into my life. Suddenly, I could attend groups without leaving my house. The world became connected in a new way and people across the country and globe could interact with each other and share space. I was able to attend events in the evening from home which I would have been unable to do before because my evening medication prevented me from driving. I began to access women's circles led by the wonderful Andrea Jackson. I was introduced to drinking ceremonial cacao, journalling and oracle cards. I was immersed in new learning, appreciation, friendships and connections with women on similar journeys to myself.

Cacao

Cacao is a plant medicine used as a health elixir and there's evidence of its use as far back as 3,900 years ago! It was used by many tribes but has great significance for the Mayans and is still an important part of their culture today. Cacao ceremonies take place during weddings and social gatherings. Mayan midwives also use it. When the Spanish colonised South America, they realised cacao's value and took it back to Europe where they added spices and sugar to sweeten it.

As it spread across the world, it eventually became the solid chocolate we know and love today. The origins, benefits and understanding of ceremonial cacao have generally been lost.

However, there has been a recent rebirth of its use in its purest form by using it as a drink and sharing space with others. Its sacredness and value are being reclaimed across the world and, in particular, in the Western world as people become more conscious of their self-awareness and the importance of how we think, feel and set our intentions.

Drinking cacao as a daily ritual, either alone or as part of a group provides sacred time to set intentions, meditate and hold space for yourself. When a group of people share cacao, there's a shared elevation of mood, increased empathy, vitality, intuition, sense of presence and opening of the heart.

The healing powers and nutrients of cacao will only be felt if 100% raw cacao is used. Processing cacao into powder removes all the healthy fats so it's best to source fair-trade cacao that is sold in a block. I purchase Oh My Goddess Ceremonial Cacao from www.radiantwoman.me as it's sourced from a small farming cooperative in Peru.

So, what are the benefits of drinking cacao? Why would you go to all that bother? Its benefits include:

- Antidepressant;
- Antioxidant;
- Plant medicine provides healing and reassurance;
- Heart opening;
- Focuses on mental clarity;
- Promotes a feeling of peacefulness;

- Contains the following minerals; calcium, copper, iron, manganese, magnesium, phosphorus, sulphur required for emotional and physical well-being;
- Good for the heart, regulating blood pressure and blood sugars; and
- Contains anandamide a neurotransmitter responsible for feeling happy and balanced.

So you've sourced your cacao - now what? Now you create a ritual. The best time to drink cacao is in the morning so that you can set your intentions for the day.

Make your cacao drink

I use:

- 10-20g of raw cacao for daily rituals but increase this to 30-40g for a ceremony in a group;
- 250ml filtered water. I have a Britta filter kettle so I use boiled water;
- 250ml plant milk - for me it's either almond, oat or coconut milk;
- Tbsp Organic honey; and
- Tsp cayenne pepper, cinnamon, sea salt.

This is quite a basic recipe but there are other ingredients that you can add such as rose water or orange water and essential oils such as cardamom, geranium, orange or spearmint. Just don't add anything artificial; everything must be pure.

Add the cacao and water to the pan and heat gently, do not allow the liquid to boil as this damages the cacao. Then add the spices, salt and finally the plant milk and honey. Use a blender to create bubbles in the liquid as these release the spirit of cacao.

Find a quiet place to sit and, if you like, you can play some relaxing music. Breathe deeply in three to four times and smell the scent of the cacao. Now comes the intention setting. As you take your first sip, give thanks for the bean. I use visualisation in my ritual; I picture the bean on the plant in its beautiful growing environment. I see the weather required for the bean to grow. With the second sip, I give thanks for the people who have nurtured and tended the plant. I visualise each part of the process from harvesting to delivery to my home. From the third sip onward, I set an intention. I repeat an intention with each sip. Here are a few of the things I might say.

"I am healed."

~

"I am calm."

~

"Today, I will hear my body and rest when needed."

~

"I have all the time I need."

I always feel calmer, more focused and grounded afterwards. Sometimes, I pull an oracle card or, if I have time, I may journal but often it's just the cacao ritual then I'm on my way for the day.

I've also been fortunate to attend the Oh My Goddess retreat in North Yorkshire twice; led by Andrea Jackson and Nicky Hollins, 40 women sharing space in a field, meditating, dancing, singing, sharing cacao and food, joining in rituals around the stone circle and creating deep friendships. What an amazing opportunity. The first year was a real catalyst for change and, during the cacao-fuelled, blindfolded spirit dance, I experienced moments of real clarity. I could see things that were holding me back, specifically things that were linked to mania. I was able to make simple changes when I got home that have helped me to not only understand myself but also to take control of my own life. I've relished each opportunity to meditate and dig deep into my soul, to learn about myself and to be empowered by that knowledge. People instructing you to do things is rarely helpful so you must seek out approaches and find your own way of doing things as only this will bring solace and calm. Whilst I have grown in these settings, what is most impactful is the personal development and change that continues long after the circles or retreats have ended.

Womb healing

When I attended the first Oh My Goddess retreat in 2021, I met Emily Webster. One evening, between activities, a group of us were chatting and Emily told us about her womb healing course. I was captivated! I'd never heard of anything like it but I felt that it would benefit me in so many ways, particularly in terms of my guilt and shame linked to my manic episodes and the things that were creating barriers and holding me back. So, after an epiphany of self-discovery on the retreat, a few months later, I signed up for womb healing and what turned out to be a very transformative journey using my newfound knowledge. It was during this course that I was compelled to share my journey, the idea for this book was born and Emily introduced me to Russell-Alexander Publishing who guided me throughout the writing process.

Purely by chance (or maybe not!), whilst writing the introduction to this section about womb healing, I found the notebook I had used during the course. Reading through it, I've been quite emotional and also struck by how far I've come since I completed the course. I delved really deep and confronted myself and my demons linked, in particular, to my behaviour during my manic episodes. The guilt and shame came up over and over during the womb healing, and exploration into my maternal ancestral line conveyed that these issues run deep in my DNA but I have the power to alter this course.

Something else that became very obvious during the womb healing sessions was the importance of language and the connotations linked to individual words. This was especially valuable when considering the language I was using to describe myself or when talking about myself. I needed to be kinder and show self-compassion. Part of this process was to accept that, when I had behaved out of character, it was due to mental illness. I was ill and that took a long time to come to terms with and accept.

In between the weekly womb healing sessions, I was able to reflect back to my manic episodes and periods of depression and I could see that there had been a lot of confusion during these times. That has definitely eased, given time and working on my own self-development, along with learning more about bipolar disorder. I have experienced depressive and manic episodes with extreme feelings associated with each, confusion about my emotions and turbulence and difficulty in organising my thoughts regarding these polarising experiences. How could I feel such guilt and shame while, at the same time, seeking the euphoria of mania? I began to understand that these feelings were not based on reality and that I owed it to myself to maintain a balanced mood that would enable me to be my authentic self, safe in the knowledge that my experiences were real.

This kind of work is not easy and it's a real challenge not to hide and avoid the really tough stuff. This was a safe and sacred space with such wonderful guidance and support from Emily as I attended the sessions and listened to the experiences of the other women. There was a release during the sessions brought on by a fearless voyage into my emotional state and this release and fresh understanding about myself continued long after the weekly sessions finished. I do think I will probably have to deal with the inner conflict that living with bipolar brings forever but my reaction and response to that conflict has changed along with acceptance and self-forgiveness. I'm definitely gentler and kinder to myself. I nurture myself with compassion and self-care. I've always been good at using these skills with others but now I use them to heal myself.

During the sessions, I experienced a cord-cutting for the first time. Cord-cutting is the severing of an unhealthy energetic relationship between you and another person, event or thing. Emily guided us through the process and it was extraordinary! My aura felt like it was vibrating and, when the sword cut the cord and I was severed from the relationship that was causing me harm, the vibration immediately stopped. I've used YouTube videos to perform cord cuttings since then but I've never experienced anything like I did during the womb healing. This experience is about protecting yourself rather than causing harm to anyone else. You are simply disconnecting your energies and connecting the other person back to the universal life force energy for their highest good. Wow! It was amazing and quite indescribable. But the real magic was yet to happen and, on reflection a couple of weeks later,

I realised that the thoughts that were holding me back had gone. I was truly disconnected from those things.

I'm always on the lookout for new women's circles and opportunities for self-development. Lots of things appeal to me but I trust my instincts and divine timing that the right thing will appear just when I need it. It always does! You can find out more about Emily's work at www.autumnblossoms.co.uk

Gather the Women

The women's circles I've attended have led me to lots of other circles and self-development courses including womb healing and Gather the Women. As soon as I heard of Gather the Women, I knew I wanted to take part in this 22-day immersion. Then I read "The Women Who Gathered" by Lynette Allen who had created the experience. This book was a collaboration of women's experiences of their 22-day journey. I knew many of them from the women's circles. The first seven days focus on the girl I used to be, the second seven days on the woman I am now and the final seven on the woman I am yet to become.

After reading the book, I was desperate to find a facilitator and embark on this journey. I began searching for an opportunity to take part. Eventually, I found Stevie Foster who was running Gather the Women on a Sunday evening. A small group of women had signed up but, one by one, they dropped out until only Stevie and I were left. I was given the option to carry on or to wait until more people signed up. I decided it was meant to be this way and so my journey began.

During the first week, I was away visiting my Gran but I ensured that I had some time every day and I packed the ingredients for my cacao, candles, art materials, oracle cards, journal and cleansing spray. Every Sunday, we met on Zoom to share cacao, meditation and our experiences from during the week. Every day, a ritual would be sent via WhatsApp and I would dedicate at least half an hour to cacao, meditation, pulling an oracle card, journalling and completing the daily ritual. The rituals were varied and creative and I valued this time to dig deep and contemplate my life so far. I celebrated myself, my achievements, my resilience, determination and sensuality. I made peace with the past and sincerely forgave myself. I gave thanks for all I had endured that had led me to where I am now and I felt proud and safe in the knowledge that I can handle whatever is yet to come. I was blessed to have learned from wise women and to have shared healing and personal growth in such a safe and sacred space.

I continue to search for more of these opportunities as I've learned the value and extreme power of them. You can learn more about Gather the Woman and Lynette's other books at www.awomansblessing.com

Mantra meditation

Through the women's circles, I was also introduced to Julie Keen who holds space and guides a group of us through a gorgeous meditation and chanted mantra on Sunday mornings. I was already aware of the power of sound healing from attending sound baths (if you haven't been to one, I can highly recommend them) but this mantra work is completely different because the sound comes from within you. Sound healing is the use of instruments, music, tones and vibrations that produce deep rest and nervous system rebalancing and can create an emotional release.

The group is such a beautiful start to the day and is powerful beyond belief. The wealth of knowledge and healing power of the women who attend this group is unbelievable. At first, some of the women I crossed paths with at women's circles, retreats and the mantra session, left me feeling intimidated but further exploration of my feelings made me understand I had mistaken intimidation for awe. I know I have so much left to learn but I recognise that I also bring my unique knowledge and power to the circles.

One member of the group once said, "Women are my medicine" which sums it up nicely. The group not only meet on a Sunday morning but they also support each other offering healing, endless support, guidance and oracle card readings on an online group. Women supporting women without judgement and full of love and respect for each other is how the world should be.

Religion

So, if you've reached this far in the book, you may be surprised to see a section on religion. Maybe you imagined I was an atheistic or agnostic. I'm a practising Christian and God is my universal lifeforce energy provider. The first place I went when I was allowed a few hours out of hospital was my church. I craved the sanctuary and the feeling of safety it provided. I needed an opportunity to talk to God, and to ask for help, support and guidance.

I moved to the area I now live in 21 years ago, heavily pregnant and doing a three-hour round trip twice a week to the antenatal diabetes clinic at the hospital near my previous home.

During this journey, I passed the most beautiful church built in the 14th century. I was so drawn to the building that I decided, that once my baby was born, I would start attending services there. So, when my son was five weeks old, I went for the first time. Since then, I've celebrated his Thanksgiving and Christening and my wedding in this sacred place. It's a very special place but, most importantly for me, I've gained a church family, friendship and endless support.

Attending services has helped to provide routine especially when I've had spells when I've been unable to work. Life is very busy at times and having split days off means that, at the moment, I'm not in church as often as I would like on a Sunday or Tuesday morning but I think Christianity is more than attending services. The disruption of Covid hasn't helped either. I try to live by the Commandments every day. In Reiki, there are five principles which blend perfectly with the Christian Commandments. I've also been heavily involved in children's ministry which allows me to utilise my teaching skills and youth work.

How does my life as a Christian fit with my life as a Reiki practitioner, crystal collector and explorer of spirituality in a wider context? The way I see it, when I'm unwell with my bipolar disorder whether that be high or low moods, I'm not the best version of myself and I can't be a good Christian either. I believe God wants me to be as well as I can be and the best version of myself to be able to follow the teachings of Christ. I'm not a good person when I'm manic. I'm selfish and my behaviour is totally out of character. I can do things that are inherently against my core values when my mood crashes and then I live with so much shame and guilt. God has provided me with so many opportunities to learn and grow to heal myself and to heal others. What a priceless gift.

I see many similarities between my Christian life and spiritual life; Communion and the Cacao ceremony; prayers said in unison in both settings; singing together; providing support for those around you and helping those less fortunate by action or through charity. Also, support and friendship; being with like-minded people who care without judgment; and moments of stillness and reflection aided by readings, poetry or images in art or on oracle cards. For me, these two worlds are not separate entities but are intrinsically linked.

I receive a daily email containing a Bible verse. The other day, I was sent Isaiah 48:17: "I am the Lord your God, who teaches you what is best for you, who directs you in the way you should go". It's written in scripture that the signs and messages I need to follow are around me. I just need to tune in and take stock of them; the direction I'm going in is clearly working and I should continue along this path.

I also had a thought the other day about crystals. God created the world (although I'm pretty sure the seven days it took aren't literally seven days. Maybe a discussion for another time). Therefore, He created the crystals in all their beauty as energy healing sources. I know some people will find my view, that Christianity and spirituality sit perfectly side by side, bizarre and that's fine but, for me, it's a perfect partnership.

I have all the
time I need

Just as it is!

Holidays

Managing your mood can be tricky at times. Even the happiest, most exciting times can be a catalyst to send your mood soaring. I've just come back from a week's holiday. The run-up to the holiday was crazy with family events and shift changes the week before as well as planning, packing and organising.

The week away in the Yorkshire Dales was fantastic, giving us time in nature and, with no timetable to follow, we just went at whatever pace we fancied. However, for much of the time, my busy brain was working overtime, knowing I had a lot to do when I got back home and I was finding it hard to slow my brain down. The most important thing was that I was aware this was happening. I still attended my mantra meditation session on Zoom and made time to practise mindfulness.

When I got back home, there was no improvement. I had a fantastic evening when we returned; my choir and the local male voice choir were doing a joint concert with songs from the sixties. It was fantastic and ended up being a late night with karaoke afterwards. That meant I took my antipsychotic medication late which had a massive impact on my ability to get to sleep. Having a buzzing brain like this could be a trigger for hypomania and I know that I must watch and track this carefully. I'm planning rest breaks and times to relax and enjoy mindful activities. I do the important stuff, prioritise and then do the rest when I get around to it and ask for help when I need it. I make lists, chat about it with friends and family and sometimes just leave things that aren't particularly important.

Sharing how I'm feeling is also really important as, if I've communicated about my overactive brain to someone, I can't deny it's happening. Being truthful in the early stages makes a massive difference to putting the brakes on and getting back to a more even mood.

I know implementing these changes works! I haven't had a manic episode for nine years but it's only possible because I know my triggers and the early warning signs, and I react quickly.

My Bipolar Tool Box

Gratitude, Affirmations & Language

Gratitude

It's very easy to focus on the negatives and the things we find overwhelming. I've found that one negative thought leads to another and soon I'm in a spiral of swirling thoughts that are affecting my mood. I know I'm privileged and have so many things to be grateful for in my life; family, friends, pets, the ability to manage my various health issues, financial security and so much more. However, at times, I need a gentle reminder to switch the negative for the positive.

In the past, I've tried various ways of recording what I'm grateful for. First, I created a positivity jar. I was so pleased to find a huge glass storage jar in a charity shop and, virtually every day, I wrote the date and a positive thing that had happened that day on a piece of A4 paper. I cut the paper into strips folded them and popped them in the jar. I managed to do this almost every day for 18 months. If I missed a day or two, I didn't worry and just started again when I remembered. The idea was that, on a difficult day or a day when I was finding it hard to come up with a positive, I could take one of the strips out and focus on that memory. I will be honest, I've never lifted a strip out of that jar but it's still on the windowsill in the living room and one day I might just see what's inside.

Next, I bought a lovely notebook with my initial on the front and each day I wrote down three things that I was grateful for. Occasionally, I would have a mental block and couldn't really think of anything specific for that particular day so, on those occasions, I would use my little list of things I have constant gratitude for, my family, my dogs and my home.

I'm great at starting daily rituals and then I'll miss a few days, then a few weeks or even months. There's no pressure and no harm done if you miss doing it for a while. Maybe being well enough and busy enough not to have the time to fill in a gratitude journal is something to be grateful for! Then I decided to do a gratitude day where I kept a notepad and pen close by and, during each task that day, I reflected on what I had at that moment to be grateful for and I then posted it on Facebook.

4/8/21 Facebook post

"So, I recently started a gratitude journal, just three things a day I was grateful for. Then I decided to have a gratitude day, to be mindful all day of things I'm grateful for not just the obvious things but the mundane things that I get fed up with when I should notice the joy in them. So, I created this list on 31/7/21 and I'm sure I will have missed a few things.

- A safe place to sleep
- A comfy bed
- A loo
- Clean sheets
- Clean running water
- A house I can share with my pets
- A garden
- Nature on my doorstep
- A washing machine I can clean my family's clothes in
- Fresh food in abundance

- Free access to medication without which I would die
- Friends I've made on walks with my dogs
- Mobile phone
- People to call
- Video messaging
- Trees and flowers
- Curiosity and interest in things
- Birds
- A job I love
- Communication skills
- Passing the time talking to strangers
- A beautiful home
- Clean washing
- Fudge and Foggy
- Planning things for the future
- Fresh fruit and veg
- Financial security
- Cuddles
- Dreams
- People who produce my food
- Food that comes from abroad
- Entertainment
- Scientists who discovered my medications
- Coffee
- Cuddles
- Candles

- A husband who is my best friend and my soulmate
- My son who is also my friend
- The ability to have borne a child
- Rubbish collections
- A family that always has my back

I then found a lovely, guided gratitude journal that I had previously bought and it invited me to record my mood and actions for the day and also a space to record what I needed to do to achieve these things. There was a section to complete at the end of each day to reflect on what I had achieved and my mood. I quickly noticed two important things; my mood was always lower in the morning than in the evening and, to achieve the actions I'd set, I was often writing about a need to take my time, completing one task before moving on to the next, breathe and be mindful. Excellent daily advice to myself!"

Affirmations

Affirmations are positive statements, thoughts or beliefs. For me, they often go hand and hand with my gratitude practices. When I first started using affirmations, I found it useful to begin with things I already believed. For example, "I am resilient'"; I knew this was true because I had overcome so much. Jumping straight in with "I am confident" would have been too difficult because, at that point, I didn't feel confident and, like so many of the other ideas and practices I've outlined in this book, starting small and building up slowly is the key. Something else I found helpful was to try to find the opposite positive phrase to a negative. If it was a rainy day, instead of dwelling on the rain, I gave thanks for the flowers and crops being watered. I think the use of affirmations and turning negatives into positives are two separate things but, for me, they are bound together. There are lots of different ways to use affirmations. You can buy cards or books, download apps, stick them up on Post-it notes or do a Google search for affirmations on a particular subject. You will find some of my favourite affirmations throughout this book. If you want to write your own affirmations, there are a few rules you should follow; always use the present tense, make them believable, make sure they reflect your priorities, keep them positive and really feel them. Start your affirmations with; I am, I feel, I have, I live or I love.

Use of Language

This has come up quite a few times as I've been writing this book in terms of the language used by professionals to describe my condition and symptoms and the use of assumptions or use of words that imply that I'm lying. This has stayed with me for a long time. I've become aware of the way expressions of gratitude and affirmations can increase positivity. I understand that my use of language against myself breeds and grows more of the same. So, if I'm talking to myself using negative words, it's highly likely that this language will create more negativity. Often, I can transpose these phrases with facts. For example, if the negative thought is "I'm stupid, no one likes me", I can redirect that thought with: "I'm not stupid because I have graduated from university on three occasions and people do like me as I have got lots of friends". Even if I'm having a bad day and I'm finding it hard to believe these truths, the facts speak for themselves.

The key, like so many things, is to notice that this is happening early on and intercept the thought. Be gentle and kind to yourself. Talk to yourself as you would to a friend or a child. Try to find a positive; this could be something you feel or just something that you can see around you. Practice makes perfect; the more you notice these negative judgments and bounce a positive back, the easier it will become.

I now use this in a lot of different scenarios. I'm always moaning that "I don't have enough time" but when I change the phrase to "I have all the time I need", I feel less stressed and more productive. I find that I actually do have all the time I need because the important tasks always get done and those that don't are generally not important. If anyone had told me the difference this would make to my life, I would have laughed at them. However, I can testify to the amazing power of a few positive words.

My Bipolar Tool Box

Sleep, Buffers, Lists & Work-Life Balance

Sleep

We spend approximately 26 years asleep! Wow! Good sleep is vital for your health and there's a close relationship between sleep and mental health. Your body is very busy when you are asleep; muscles and tissues are repaired and immune function is increased. Poor mental health can cause sleep problems and vice versa. Everyone can relate to a night spent tossing and turning, seeing every hour on the clock and then feeling dreadful the next day. You feel grumpy and irritable, everything seems to take longer and you can't relax.

It's a complicated balance at times and it's really important, particularly when you have a condition like bipolar disorder, to prioritise a good sleep pattern. Lack of sleep can be a symptom of hypomania and mania but can also be the trigger for these episodes. I told you it was complicated. When I was first diagnosed, I was managing on a few hours' sleep each night but I had excess energy during the day. If I know I'm having disrupted sleep because of a late night out, for example, I make sure that the nights before and after are protected, that I can take my medication on time and maybe even plan a lie-in to catch up on lost sleep. Sleep disturbances are also associated with depressive episodes and insomnia (difficulty falling or staying asleep) or hypersomnia (over-sleeping) can occur.

Once a sleep pattern is disrupted, it can be hard to get back on track. It's also difficult at times in our house because my husband's sleep pattern and mine can differ. I'm sure lots of couples can relate to this. It's really difficult to keep to the routine at times. I have a few nights each week when I take my medication late due to work and hobbies and, even though I vow to keep to the schedule that I've set myself for the rest of the week, I don't always manage to. In saying that, when we went on holiday this year we still kept roughly to our usual pattern because I know it makes such a difference. All the fresh Yorkshire Dales air definitely helped too.

There's some excellent information and resources on the Mind website including some top tips if you are struggling with sleep. I've made a list of what helps me and also suggestions that the experts always recommend. We are all individuals so what works for you won't necessarily work for someone else and if, like me, you find keeping to your schedule tricky, don't worry as there's always tomorrow night when you can try again. Sweet dreams!

Things that help me

- Keeping to a regular bedtime;
- Going to bed calm;
- Having a comfy bed;
- Taking medication on time;
- Being warm enough but not too warm;
- Monitoring caffeine intake during the day;
- Keeping my blood sugars stable: this, for me, is a Type 1 Diabetes issue but I'm sure eating something sugary before bed isn't helpful for anyone;
- Listening to a podcast: if I can't sleep, this helps my brain

focus on something rather than my thoughts which will probably spiral in the quiet of the night. Also, I'm only stimulating one of my senses and still resting. I rarely get to listen to the end of a podcast;

- Using a sunshine alarm clock in the winter; and
- Taking some "me" time: when I take Foggy down for a wee at 6.45 am/7 am, I don't go back to bed. Instead, if I don't have to start getting ready for work, I have a cup of tea, read a chapter of my book and gradually wake up.

The Experts' suggestions

- Going to sleep at the same time each night and waking at the same time each morning;
- Winding down before bed; bath, reading, meditating, turning off the lights;
- Avoiding naps during the day;
- Keeping the bedroom for sleep and sex, limiting TV and mobile devices in the bedroom;
- Avoiding alcohol and caffeine;
- Avoiding large meals before bed; and
- Leaving a gap of a few hours between any exercise and bedtime.

Buffers

What is a buffer? To me, a buffer is a technique I use before and/or after an anxiety-inducing activity. For example, if I know I'm going to be in the car as a passenger, I'm much less anxious if I get into the car when I'm in a calm state. Beforehand, I can meditate, walk the dogs, sit mindfully with a cup of tea, etc. I may still need to use strategies when I'm travelling and when I arrive at my destination, I may need to repeat a buffer from before the journey by doing another activity or I may not need another buffer at all. It varies a lot. Time is always a factor as, if it's limited, I may have to do something quickly like a breathing technique or, if I have plenty of time, a long walk instead.

Buffers also help me manage my chronic pain and the fatigue that comes with it. Sometimes it involves mapping out my entire week so that I have opportunities to rest or enjoy restful activities like reading or soaking in a bubble bath. All this self-care has become necessary for me to manage my mood and my pain levels. For a long time, it felt selfish and self-indulgent until I realised that it was vital for my physical and mental health and so I changed the language I used around these buffers.

If something is causing me anxiety, I score it out of ten. Let's imagine I have a stressful hospital appointment. It's seven out of ten on my anxiety score. Before I leave the house, I have a drink so that I'm not dehydrated which will probably contribute to the anxiety symptoms. I close my eyes and do a body scan to identify where the tension is in my body and I do some breathing exercises. My anxiety score is now three out of ten. Excellent! Off to the hospital I go. In the waiting room, I notice that my anxiety levels have risen slightly so I repeat the breathing. I go into the appointment which isn't as bad as I anticipated so I might not need a post-appointment buffer at all or I might treat myself to a comforting spice chai latte (a hug in a mug) and a gentle walk just to remove any residual anxiety. A little self-praise is always good here too, something along the lines of "Well done, you made good choices and controlled your anxiety with positive self-care."

Imagine this scenario again but without the buffers. Starting with my anxiety at level seven but I'm not doing anything to tackle it or reduce it. It might go down a little, if I'm lucky, just from the distraction of the journey or reading the posters or a newspaper in the waiting room. If it doesn't reduce on its own, it may stay where it is or, if I get swept away in it and give it some attention, it may become worse. Sometimes, if I add a buffer before and/or after, I can minimise or eradicate the anxiety completely. If this isn't possible, it's still much better to walk into the appointment or any situation with a three on the anxiety scale rather than a seven. The anxiety may well rise a little anyway because the situation is stressful but three rising to five is better than seven rising to nine as the lower the anxiety, the easier it will be to tackle and stop. It's taken time and practice to work out which things help the most in different situations and also to identify when I need a buffer. It's often just by thinking about what the issue is and what I can do to help, choosing a strategy to put in place so that I'm empowered by the control I have over things and reminding myself that these techniques have been successful for me in the past.

Lists

I love lists. Whenever I'm feeling overwhelmed or if I have a lot to remember, I make a list. Paper lists, lists on my phone and lists on the whiteboard in my kitchen. I've always relied on lists to help me be productive and effective and to act as an aid to my memory. Lists have become a vital tool in managing my mental health as my memory is not what it was. I'm also not sure if this is due to "bipolar brain", as I like to call it, or if it's the side effects of my medication. Either way, the cause is irrelevant but having a way to minimise the damage of forgetting things is essential.

When I'm feeling stressed or when I have lots to do and don't know where to start, I simply make a hot decaf drink, sit down for five minutes and make a list of what needs to be done. This promotes calmness, I'm able to do one job at a time instead of multitasking badly and I'm more productive as I work on the priority jobs first. Often, there are a few things left undone and that's okay because the important stuff always gets taken care of. I menu plan every week and create a shopping list based on the plan. It's really useful to work out which evenings I need to make something quick and on other evenings I can cook something that needs more preparation and cooking time. "Fend for yourself" evenings are a recent addition to take the pressure off me and, on those evenings, my husband and son have to prepare their own tea.

I have lists on my phone that I re-use year after year such as the Christmas presents list. I sometimes make a positive "done" list so I can see what I've actually achieved and this goes a long way to fending off any negative thoughts about the day's achievements. Also, I sometimes create a "to-do" list comprising only those activities that I want to do for my mental well-being, such as yoga, meditation, journaling, reading, etc. I treat myself to menu planners, cute Post-it notes, funky pens and other stationery that I like to use. All these things make my lists more fun and easier to follow.

Finding a Work-Life Balance

Before I became unwell, I was a full-time special needs teacher. I absolutely loved my job and I have no doubt that, had I not become unwell, I would still be teaching today. The universe had other ideas! For 18 months after my hospital admission, I was still employed as a teacher but was off work on long-term sick leave. I was a shadow of my former self and I felt lost. It became apparent that going back to work in the school was not a viable option. A lot of my mania had been played out at work and I was ashamed and embarrassed by my uncharacteristic behaviour. Even the thought of visiting the school was unbearable. I had panic attacks and my emotional state caused episodes of self-harm and dissociation. Losing my job due to my ill health was devastating but was also an opportunity to close the door on that part of my life and look to the future. I was able to dedicate more time to my recovery without the worry of returning to work hanging over my head.

During that period of unemployment, I began to build a routine for myself. This included attending church on Tuesday mornings, joining a gardening group near my home and volunteering for a charity that provided adult literacy and numeracy lessons for people with learning disabilities. I met new people and used many of the skills I thought were lost forever. I gained confidence, self-esteem and self-respect. I made a difference in my own life and the lives of others.

It soon became apparent that I had made enough progress in my recovery to be able to take on some paid work. I saw an advertisement for a job with a charity supporting adults with learning disabilities. It was local and the contract was for 15 hours a week. Start slowly and build up gradually, I thought. However, in this particular situation, being honest about my mental health status from the beginning was not a good idea. I rarely worked 15 hours as that contract didn't really exist. The job wasn't right for me but it wasn't long before an exciting opportunity came up. So, I ended up working for a different charity and being responsible for arranging youth clubs and events for young people with learning disabilities. This job was exciting and I attacked it with the enthusiasm I had felt when I was teaching. After my bad experience at the last job, after disclosing my mental health status, I decided to keep it a secret this time. Unfortunately, I hadn't been there long when I started to become unwell and my second manic episode began. Working until late in the evenings and being responsible for both the young people, a large staff team and an even larger team of volunteers contributed to this and I ended up leaving without giving a full explanation as to the reason. Whilst these two jobs weren't the right fit for me, they taught me invaluable lessons that I would need if I was to keep my bipolar stable.

Firstly, disclosure of my condition is in everyone's best interests. If, after I've disclosed my bipolar disorder, I'm penalised and victimised, they don't deserve me. I'm worth more and should work in a place that respects me. I will leave and look for something else. Also, working long hours or late into the evening does not suit me, especially as my medication schedule and a good sleep routine are vital for my bipolar to remain stable. Being in charge, especially of a team of staff, is too much for me now. Being a lone worker now suits my needs.

Speaking up and advocating for what I need is vital. This skill has the power to prevent me from becoming unwell in the first place. Prevention is always better than recovery.

Voluntary work gives me a sense of purpose, improves my self-esteem and allows me to give back to my community. Without volunteers, the UK would fall apart so, if you aren't well enough to do paid work, you should be proud and empowered by your ability to contribute within the voluntary sector.

I now have a work schedule that, on paper, looks like it wouldn't work for a person with bipolar disorder: three jobs, one evening and one long day. Everyone who employs me knows about my mental health. Each job is rewarding and uses a wide variety of my skills so I feel fulfilled. I have good support at home and at work so any issues with my mental health are recognised early and the support I need to rebalance is provided quickly and without question. If work feels too much at any time, I have lots of non-working time in my week to ensure that I'm using the strategies and techniques I need to level myself out.

Just as it is!

Coping with the Summer Heat

The weather is super-hot. It's beyond hot and there's a weather warning. Now, as much as I would like my legs to tan to the same colour as my arms, I'm not lying out on my sun lounger soaking up the rays. Instead, I'm keeping cool in the house using the fan and wet flannels. The reason for this is because I'm worried. Heat like this can easily cause dehydration. Dehydration for people on lithium therapy can be deadly. Dehydration can cause the levels of lithium to rise in the bloodstream and this can cause lithium toxicity. Signs of lithium toxicity include hyper-extension of the limbs, toxic psychosis, renal failure, seizures, electrolyte imbalance, dehydration, circulatory failure, coma and death. Scary list! It's always at the forefront of my mind in weather like this. I also discovered, when researching lithium toxicity, that some people are at greater risk. This includes people with hypertension, diabetes, congestive heart failure, chronic renal disease, schizophrenia and Addison's disease.

Great! So I have Type 1 Diabetes too. My diabetic control is also affected by the heat so this can feel like a hopeless situation. It's not hopeless though. I know it takes a lot of extra work, planning and care but I am able to make good choices and put self-care at the top of my agenda. That means lots of water, fresh fruit and vegetables that have high water content, staying out of the sun and, if I do go out, having plenty of water with me and minimising my time outside as much as possible.

Socially Acceptable Drugs

This may well turn out to be one the shortest chapters of this book but it may also contain the most powerful information about things I became aware of early on in my journey; things that have made a phenomenal difference in my life, particularly in drastically reducing my anxiety levels.

Caffeine

I do love a hot drink, especially a good quality coffee from a nice independent coffee shop. In fact, I'm currently sitting in one such coffee shop as I'm writing this chapter! I'm in Rivers Meet and I've sat here many times writing, first my dissertation and then this book. During my first period of sick leave from work, when I was diagnosed with PTSD but not yet with bipolar disorder, I was agoraphobic. Leaving the house was possible but incredibly difficult and I minimised it as much as possible. Most days, I only managed the school run and, even then, I didn't always get out of the car and often spent most of my day in my bedroom where I felt safer.

I also drank a lot of coffee and, as soon as my mug was empty, the kettle was back on. This was a massive increase in my previous coffee consumption when I was working. I continued like this for months. I'm not really sure when I made the connection between my coffee intake and my constant shaking and moderate levels of constant anxiety that sometimes peaked but never came down to a low or non-existent level. Then, one day, I had a lightbulb moment. I needed to reduce my caffeine intake. I went cold turkey which was really tough as I had headaches for two weeks and felt even more dreadful, if that was possible. Reducing caffeine intake gradually over an extended period may be a kinder way to reduce or remove caffeine from your life. It's difficult to adequately describe the vast difference this made to my life; the shakes reduced, my anxiety levels lowered and it was easier for me to identify my anxiety triggers. I also felt like I had regained some control. I was making positive changes and it was working.

It's only now, while writing and reflecting on that time, that I can see that implementing that simple change and the direct and positive impact it had on my life, must have been the catalyst for me to make more changes. Empowering!

Sleep can be an absolute nightmare when you are struggling with mental illness, either too much or not enough, but too much caffeine will definitely not help so you may also see an improvement in your sleep if you reduce your caffeine intake. You don't need to deny yourself your favourite cuppa; just swap to a decaffeinated brand instead. For me, now, it's caffeine in the morning to give me a boost as I'm so groggy because of my medication. Then, I have decaffeinated after lunch but if I'm out and about, unless it's in the evening, I rarely remember to ask for decaf. This balance has been working well for me but, recently, I limited myself to decaffeinated for eight weeks and I found that I had a lot more energy. This may have been the lack of caffeine or a change in my diet, who knows? What I do know is that too much caffeine does not sit well with me at all and I must limit my intake.

Alcohol

Why does it seem acceptable now to drink alcohol daily or in vast quantities? This doesn't have anything to do with what I'm about to share with you but lots of shops now sell trinkets, money boxes, slogan art, etc., with slogans such as "Gin O'clock" or

"Mum's Prosecco Fund". What's that all about? There are better options for de-stressing at the end of the day.

I was never a big drinker or a daily drinker. As a student, yes, I drank more alcohol. When I found out I was pregnant, I didn't drink at all apart from a sip of champagne at my university graduation four weeks before I gave birth to my son. I would have a glass of wine on a Friday evening, the bottle was left in the fridge until it was undrinkable, like vinegar a few weeks later, so it went down the sink. I swapped to the individual bottles of wine soon after. I would perhaps drink a little more at Christmas. I hated that out-of-control feeling of being drunk, alcohol sent my blood sugars a bit loopy and hangovers sucked!

Fast forward to mentally unwell Laura. I wasn't drinking more than usual or using alcohol to self-medicate. I noticed that after my mum's 60th birthday party and a night out a few weeks beforehand with my brother when I drank more than usual, on both occasions, my world fell apart afterwards. At this point, I was diagnosed with PTSD but not bipolar disorder. My depression was so severe that self-harm increased and I couldn't manage more than a few simple daily tasks. It was incredibly debilitating. Again, I had this lightbulb moment of self-awareness, that acknowledgement of the link between alcohol and mental instability. I stopped drinking right then.

Fast forward five months and, by this time, I'd been in hospital for a month and was gradually learning to live in the real world again. My husband took me away for a spa weekend in Chester. We had a lovely time and it was just what we needed but, on the last night, I had an alcoholic milkshake, yes that is a thing! The next day, I was tearful and anxious and my mood dropped. Luckily, we were going home that day so it didn't spoil the trip.

I haven't had an alcoholic drink since then and that was over 12 years ago. I can honestly say that I don't miss it. My friends are great when we go out and there has never been pressure to drink. I'm open about the reasons why I abstain and everyone is accepting of it. It also means that I can be the designated driver and give people lifts. Oh, and no hangovers! Of course, there are the odd occasions, such as Christmas and holidays abroad, when I think maybe I could try just having one but the fear of the repercussions and the possibility, no matter how slight, that I could fall back into the black hole of despair and depression just isn't worth it.

My medical records state, "denies having a problem with drink". I hate that statement. I never had a problem with alcohol, it just exasperated my symptoms and I chose to make a lifestyle change that aided my recovery. I found it an easy change to make and I know I'm really lucky with that. However, if you believe that it's going to be a challenge to make this change or even to start by reducing your alcohol intake, there's lots of help and support out there. You don't have to do it alone.

The first step for me, with both caffeine and alcohol, was admitting there was a connection between them and my mental health symptoms. Then I found the self-motivation to change and I'm incredibly glad that I did. I definitely wouldn't be as well as I am now if I hadn't committed to reducing and eliminating caffeine and alcohol from my life. I have recently discovered non-alcoholic wine which tastes just like normal wine and it's a lovely alternative to the bottled grape juice that pretends to be wine. There's a wide range of alcohol-free alternatives on the market now. I choose one of those or a drink I wouldn't normally have – just for a change. Cloudy lemonade? Yes, please!

Just as it is!

MRI scan

I needed another MRI scan of my leg to see if there was anything that was causing the constant pain after breaking it in four places. The first MRI had caused me to be really anxious, possibly due to fear of the unknown. With hindsight, and now having had two MRIs, I now think my anxiety was actually linked to PTSD and the thought of being trapped in the car. I'm not sure exactly where that thought comes from as neither car accident caused me to be trapped but a lot of my fear came from the "what if's." Anyway, back to the scan. I felt anxious before I left the house and this increased when I got into the waiting room. I then had to change to another waiting room and the nurse who showed me the way asked how I was. I was completely honest and explained I was feeling anxious and that I knew there was nothing to worry about as I had previously had a scan but I was struggling. "We can put you into the scanner legs first so your whole body doesn't need to go in," she said. This sounded like it would help me feel a bit better.

While I was sitting in the waiting room, I tried some breathing exercises. I persevered for a while but didn't feel I was properly focused. Instead of ploughing on with something that wasn't helping very much, I changed to reading everything on the walls. Then someone else came into the waiting room and we had a quick chat. This definitely distracted me so I was calmer going into the scanner room.

I got onto the table but they had forgotten I was to go into the scanner feet first. Next came some positive self-talk “It’s just a noisy machine, “Close your eyes and focus on something else” and “You’ve done this before.” Then I had to come out of the scanner because I was still wearing my bra and it was underwired! They put me back in, feet first, and off we went again.

For the first scan, I was wearing headphones and the radio was playing but that didn’t happen this time. So, in my head, I sang my upcoming solo for choir and, by the time I got to the end, I was calm. The scan had finished and I had developed a new mindfulness activity for myself.

The scanner was in the car park so I didn’t go back into the main hospital for a chocolate treat, as planned. I felt a little wobbly but the anxiety level was low. I did ring my mum for a chat though (another favourite de-stressing strategy of mine). I guess the lesson here was to keep going and try different things. I have lots of strategies in my mental health toolbox and I know that one will definitely work but I might have to dig deep and root around at the bottom for it. Sharing how you are feeling is helpful too.

Dogs, Hobbies & Other Distractions

Dogs...

Fudge helped save my life! This is not an over-exaggeration - he literally did. Neither my husband nor I had dogs growing up. I had a friend with a dog who pined for me every day for two weeks when I was in hospital after being diagnosed with Type 1 Diabetes. He stood by the door and cried at the time I usually called for my friend on the way to school. It was a real appreciation that a dog really was man's best friend even if it wasn't my dog and I was reminded of this experience regularly as I got older. During the first Covid lockdown in 2020, I was off work and I used some of that time to write three blog posts, one of which was about dogs:

"I suppose my love of dogs started when I was 12. I was hospitalised for two weeks after being diagnosed with Type 1 Diabetes. Tom, a Collie, sat at my friend's front door every morning at a quarter past eight pining for me when I should have been calling on my way to the bus stop. It was a really difficult time for me and I was so touched to hear about Tom's reaction to my absence.

"Fast forward 20 years, when a chance interaction on Twitter about an Olympic torch made out of a Pringles tube began a special friendship. A short time after, this new friend got a Labrador puppy and closely watching those early days and the progress they made together was heartwarming and inspiring. At that time, I was desperately trying to conceive baby number two. Years had gone by and I had been unable to fall pregnant. Getting a puppy seemed like it would fill a void in my heart. Encouraged by my friend, who said things like “Get a puppy. It will be good for your son” “You won’t regret it”, I started my search. It took six months of research into different breeds to decide as this wasn’t a decision to be taken lightly. Then we saw an advertisement for a litter of Westiepoos. I made enquiries and my son and I went to meet the owner and the litter. Then fate stepped in. We wanted a boy and there was only one left so he was destined to be ours. Two weeks later, in April 2013, we went to collect Fudge and our family was complete.

“Sometimes in life, things don’t hit you at the time. A 52-seater coach crashed into my car in 2011. I was calm and collected in the immediate aftermath and just carried on. It happened during the half-term holiday so I didn’t take any time off work. Life seemed to continue as usual, except the trauma of that stormy night created a storm in me that gradually picked up pace and made me very unwell. I became so unwell I had to give up work. I spent more and more time with Fudge, my constant companion. Not only was he with me 24/7, but he was also completely dependent on me, my reason to get up and exercise twice a day, to get me out in the fresh air and see fellow dog walkers and stop to pass the time of day. He needed me to be there, so I was. My love for him was so deep and unconditional that he, alongside my family, provided me with a drive to get well and he nurtured my ability to practise self-care.

“Dog walks became more mindful as I noticed the ever-changing seasons, saw the buds bursting open and the leaves falling from the trees and crunching underfoot. No matter what the weather, I was out walking and my physical health definitely improved. I rarely have a cold now. Those dog walkers I met became a group of friends who I go out with socially and some very close friends who I can rely on no matter what and who know I’m always there for them too. Over time, I got better, learned new skills and refocused my purpose in life, but that's the content for my next blog.

"Previously, I didn't appreciate that my mental wellness should have been a priority – I do now. Fudge remains a vital part of my mental wellness, creating the need for a routine and the dependency he will always have on me. This year, after a lot of discussion with my husband, we adopted Foggy, an ex-breeder. It was time to give back to the dog world what Fudge had given to us, making good use of not only the seven years' experience as dog owners looking after Foggy but also the experience of struggling with anxiety and being able to relate to her in a way I couldn't have done when we got Fudge. It's still early days but she's making great progress and underpinning that is the same routine and structure that helped me get back on my feet and continues to help me remain grounded and well today."

At that point in my life, I wasn't ready to write about my bipolar disorder or even name it but the truth is that "really unwell" doesn't begin to describe the severity of what I was going through. Fudge was by my side through it all. His dependency forced me to get up and keep to the routine that he needed. I was mum to a twelve-year-old at the time of my diagnosis and my son needed me too. He was obviously a key driving force for me to keep going no matter how dire things became. However, he was independent in many ways and Fudge was not.

There's lots of research into the effect dogs and other animals can have on your mental health. I particularly like this list that's part of an article on www.mentalhealth.org.uk

"Caring for a pet can help our mental health in many ways, including:

- increasing your physical activity. - Dog owners are likely to take their pets for a walk or run every day. This can be a fun way to fit exercise into your routine;
- providing companionship. - Pets can give you a sense of security and someone to share the day with. Caring for them can help you feel wanted and needed. This can be especially valuable for older people or those who live alone;
- reducing anxiety. - The companionship of a pet can help to ease your anxiety;
- boosting self-confidence. Pets can be great listeners, offer unconditional love and won't criticise you. This can help your self-confidence, especially if you feel isolated or misunderstood;
- helping you meet new people. - Dog owners often stop and chat with each other on walks. But other pets can be a way to meet people too: in pet shops, training classes or online groups, for example; and
- adding structure to your day. - Feeding, exercising and caring for a pet can help you keep to a daily routine, which can help you feel more grounded and focused. It can give your day purpose and a sense of achievement."

Yes, yes, yes! I 100% agree with everything on this list and have experienced it all.

Physical activity

I often wake up feeling groggy due to my antipsychotic medication but being hit by the fresh air during my morning walk instantly clears my head. I'm lucky to live in a place with lovely green spaces and trees, lots of fellow dog walkers who always say hello and lots of wildlife. There have even been deer spotted in the field by my house but I've not seen them myself yet; I'm hoping I will soon. It's actually quite amazing as I can hear the M62 from my house and I live on a very large housing estate. We also have a heron on our estate, a breeding pair of egrets and apparently mink!

A five-minute drive away from my home, I can be walking along the river, gazing at fields of horses, cattle and sheep along with passing barges and lots of trees. I feel truly blessed to have this beauty around me and being in nature definitely improves my mood on the day and for days afterwards. Some days, we do short walks and other days we walk a long way; the length of the walk doesn't matter as they really boost my well-being.

Companionship

My dogs are my babies and need lots of care but they are very clever and tune in to those times when I'm sad or struggling to bring my mood up. They recognise these times and come to me for a cuddle. The sensory feedback from stroking their fur, they are both incredibly soft and fluffy, is a mindful activity that I find incredibly soothing and the dogs like it too. A head resting on your knee or a toy brought to you to play and distract you is always a welcome diversion from negative thoughts. The release of oxytocin in my brain, the same hormone that forms the bond between a mother and baby, is released causing me to experience those warm fuzzy feelings. We could all do with more of them. It's no wonder the feeling of love for our pets can be so intense. My love for Fudge, who slept on my chest as an eight-week-old puppy, and the intensity of my feelings for Foggy, as we watched a closed-off, frightened and abused little dog come back to life again, is almost impossible to put into words - it's so impassioned.

Reducing Anxiety

With my dogs, I have dog snuggles, someone to talk to and share my feelings with in total confidence and it's a welcome distraction which helps to lower my anxiety. I benefit from fresh air, exercise, distraction, time in nature and socialising with the people I meet. All these things may help individually but the combination of them all can reduce my anxiety for hours, days or even weeks. I don't suffer from much anxiety and the regularity of life with the dogs definitely helps with this. High levels of stress, for example, my son's GCSE revision or lack of revision as was often the case, got my blood pressure soaring. Whenever I was really stressed out, I would pop Fudge in the car and take a short trip to the local RSPB nature reserve to breathe in that fresh air and see the beauty of nature around me, while Fudge ran off the lead loving being outside too. Pure heaven! Result: instant stress relief and a general sense of well-being.

Boosting Self Confidence

As my skills as a dog owner grew, so did my self-confidence in that area and this spilled over into other areas of my life. Knowing I could use my relationship with Fudge to tackle my anxiety demons was empowering and, with time, I began to acknowledge my part in controlling my mental health symptoms. I had lost my sense of identity and was a shadow of my former self and chatting to other dog owners and gradually developing a small group of really close friendships helped improve my confidence. People complimented me on my dog and wanted to spend time with me. This has grown even more since we adopted Foggy. My instincts in what to do with her and how to support her were utilised and, by this point, I was also a Reiki practitioner so I was able to use that skillset to bond with her and help her to heal. I had real belief in myself and I trusted and followed my instincts.

Meeting new people

From the friends I made walking the dogs on the hill near my home, to the people I only speak to on a single occasion, having the dogs has given me the opportunity to chat; chat about dogs, life, family, the environment and very occasionally politics or current affairs. My friendships with fellow dog owners have literally spread worldwide thanks to social media. I have a beautiful friend in America who has become a pen pal. We met through Instagram because we both own Westiepoos who have their own accounts! Not sure if the dogs will ever meet but hopefully the humans may - one day. I'm still in touch with the lovely lady who encouraged me to get Fudge ten years after our first interaction on Twitter around the time of the London 2012 Olympics. A little closer to home, I've been able to join local Westie walks that I discovered on Facebook. I have a great group of friends at Leeds Westie Walks and, at our monthly meet-ups, there are often 35 Westies running about together. Westie Heaven! It brings pure joy to my heart and has also given me friends for life. There are Westie walks all over the UK, some of which have a massive turnout.

Adding structure to your day

Having a good routine is important for good mental health regardless of whether you have a mental illness or not. It's also very important for dogs to have a routine and structure. Fudge and Foggy have built-in timers; morning - breakfast and walk, tea at 5 pm (they start demanding at 4.30 pm), supper is approximately 7 pm after we have had our tea but, if we eat our tea earlier, they demand their supper when we have finished, even if they have already eaten. Once Foggy gets out of her basket in the morning, she must be taken downstairs to go out for a wee; if not, she still tinkles on the carpet. I've discovered that if I make a hot drink and go back upstairs but don't snuggle back down for an extra hour's sleep, I am fresher and it's a nice relaxing way to start the day. I get myself dressed and organised, feed the dogs, walk the dogs then, if it's a workday, off I go. In the evening, I come home from work, walk the dogs, feed the dogs then start to cook our tea. It's boring, it's essential, it's structure and it's reassuring that each day has fixed things in it that keep me going. On paper, it might appear that all this was really easy to implement. I can assure you it wasn't. It took time to build up to this and a regular sleep pattern and taking my medication at the same time every evening also plays a vital role in this system. It is a system and it takes all the individual cogs to keep it moving. If anything becomes sluggish or stops working, the entire system can come crashing down very quickly. I found that starting small and making manageable, achievable changes to my routine, and then building on these when I had embedded them into my routine, was the only way to go about establishing the routine. If you try to do too much too quickly then you will probably fail. It's a marathon, not a sprint.

Of course, dogs are a huge commitment and there's a cost implication too so it's not going to be a good choice for everyone. If it's specifically a dog you would like to spend time with, there are other options such as the charity "The Cinnamon Trust" (www.cinnamon.org.uk) who are amazing. They support disabled, elderly or unwell people who are finding it difficult to walk their dogs by providing them with a volunteer dog walker. This adds an extra mental health boost for the volunteers as they are making a difference or contributing to making a difference to someone's life and also having social interaction with the dog owner. Borrow My Doggy (www.borrowmydoggy.com) is another wonderful scheme where you can help someone out by walking or looking after their dog. Lots of fun without the commitment or financial pressure of dog ownership. Or, if that's not for you, just go for a walk around your local park and say hello to the dogs you meet.

Maybe you're not a dog person at all. I've never had a cat but they are also amazing companions that give fabulous snuggles and don't need to be walked every day. Speak to any cat owner and I'm sure they will tell you a million other reasons why they would recommend a cat as a pet. A pet of any kind can boost your mental health. You have to nurture and care for it. I have friends with snakes, amphibians, goats, horses, chinchillas, degus, and even a tarantula! If you love them, they all will create a similar effect and boost those feel-good hormones. There are lots of brilliant local farms, even city farms if you're not in a rural area, where you can get up close to animals. "Be a farmer for the day" experiences, lamb feeding and petting areas are all good options if you don't want a pet of your own and the commitment that brings. There's an alpaca farm near me where you can even go alpaca trekking.

You don't even have to leave your home for some wonderment at nature. There are some fascinating nature programmes about animals in their natural habitats on TV and series about farms and pets. A tank of fish can be mindful and beautiful to watch and you can even do this on YouTube if you don't want to get real fish. Alternatively, you can simply find a nice place to sit and watch the birds out of the window for a few minutes. Calming and enjoyable.

As a teenager, I volunteered at a local animal sanctuary. I had an adopted pony and, whilst I couldn't ride him, spending hours at the stables and helping care for the animals was great fun and very rewarding. My brother also adopted an animal there; a sheep called Larry that he took for walks on a dog lead! There are animal charities all over the UK and elsewhere. Many are desperate for volunteers and struggle to operate without them. It's a great way to give back, spend some time with animals, make a difference and make new friends of both the animal and human variety.

I'd like to introduce you to a very special dog who really helps boost my mood especially if it's low. Pumpkin is a Westie (of course she is!) and she's paralysed due to extreme trauma which broke her spine. She's not in pain, she feels nothing and is doubly incontinent. She uses a wheelchair which she zips about in, happy, busy, explorative and because she has no idea that she's disabled, it doesn't stop her from doing anything! Did I mention she is incredibly cute? Her injury has meant that she hasn't grown to the size of a normal Westie. She's dinky and that just adds to her adorability and personality.

I first became aware of Pumpkin and her story through some of the Westie Facebook groups I belong to. The family that fostered her at eight weeks old, after her injury, fell head over heels in love with her and she became a part of their family. It takes a very special family to be able to provide the additional care a dog like Pumpkin needs and her family are very special indeed providing hydrotherapy, physiotherapy, nappy changes, including in the middle of the night every night, and a million other things. Pumpkin and her family are totally awesome. Pumpkin's mum posts lots of content on social media about Pumpkin's adventures with lots of photos and videos which brighten my day enormously. Last winter, I was functional but my mood was low for much of the time and every video of Pumpkin lifted my spirits, reminded me that life is for living to the full, that boundaries are meant to be broken and, no matter how small you are, it's completely achievable.

Pumpkin's family share those values and really wanted to help and support other animals with disabilities so they set up the Pumpkin and Friends charity. They have raised a phenomenal amount of money in a relatively short time and I know that, by the time this book goes to print it, they will have raised well over £200k! Pumpkin has trained to be a PAT (Pets as Therapy) dog and she regularly visits care homes and schools in her local area. The photos showing the connection and love shared between Pumpkin and the residents at the care home have brought tears of joy to my eyes at times. Even people with dementia or difficulty communicating light up when they meet Pumpkin. It's inspiring and great to see the difference one little dog can make to so many people.

I was beside myself with joy in April 2022 when I went to the York Westie Walk. This is the largest Westie walk I've attended with approximately 60 Westies in attendance each year. I love this walk but, best of all, this year I got to meet Pumpkin and her family. I even got some cuddles from her until she very clearly decided she'd had enough and wanted to scoot about with the other dogs as she was having some time out of her wheelchair. Then I had the joy of watching her play with the other dogs and their total acceptance of her.

I've continued to follow her adventures on social media and it also made me reflect on the choices I make regarding how and with whom I interact on the internet. Being in lots of groups online, and engaging in content that lifts my spirits and makes me feel good is very useful. I know I can go on Facebook or Instagram at any time and I'm unlikely to see negative things. If I do see something I don't like, I can choose not to engage and just scroll past. I like and follow things that I'm interested in; photographers who take stunning scenic photographs, lots of content with dogs, authentic and inspiring celebrities or anything else I see that makes me smile. I can't avoid what's happening in the real world, nor would I want to, but it's always about making a choice, checking in with myself and working out what my emotional self can cope with on any given day. This is something I've learned the hard way. When I'm very low and watching particular things on tv or looking at certain things on social media, I can aggravate an already bad situation or I can find something that relaxes me or makes me laugh. If in doubt, I just check Pumpkin's posts for the day and know I will get an instant lift!

Hobbies and Other Distractions

I am one of those people who likes to be busy and I recharge my batteries by being with people. This conflicts with the other people in my household who recharge by being alone. Extroverts vs Introverts! It's important for me to have a range of hobbies. They help with my routine and they bring me joy. I do have some singular activities like building Lego and relaxing with a good crime thriller but time with friends, having a nice coffee or more structured events are really important to me. When I first came out of the hospital after my diagnosis, it was scary for me to embark on new adventures. I didn't know what might have the potential to trigger manic episodes and my family were terrified of me becoming unwell again.

Every year, at our church carol service, the ladies choir based in the village would sing a few songs. The acoustics in our church are amazing and the singing often brought me to tears. Quite a few ladies from our church congregation were in the choir so there were people who had known me for many years and who knew how ill I had been. It was deemed by my family to be a "safe" activity, so I joined. It's such a great group of women and singing is definitely good for my soul. We do lots of concerts in a variety of settings, we have raised over £10,000 for Yorkshire Air Ambulance and, of course, there is our weekly rehearsal.

The success of joining the choir with no negative impact on my mood provided me and my family with the confidence to let me explore other activities. Some were linked to church like becoming a Messy Church leader and helping to create the memorial garden in the churchyard.

Volunteering in a local community garden near where I lived got me out in the fresh air and I met like-minded people. This activity stopped when I returned to paid employment but it's left me with happy memories and a sense of achievement.

The dogs have introduced me to the wonders of Westie walks; a walk in a beautiful setting followed by coffee and cake and, of course, lots of chatting. I don't get to as many walks as I would like as I work one day each weekend and the constant pain in my leg makes motorway driving difficult. However, those I do attend bring me great joy and boost me mentally for days afterwards. I've also made some special lifelong friends.

Some of the other activities I do regularly aren't hobbies as such but they are definitely distractions that quieten my busy brain. A lot of these involve my phone or tablet; online jigsaw puzzles, sudoku and gem matching puzzles, for example, help pass some time and also provide focus. I do have to monitor my time spent on these activities as I have noticed that, when my mood is low, I will tend to increase the time spent on devices. Early on, when I was learning about my condition and what did and didn't help, I noticed that when my mood was low and anxiety levels were high, too much time on my tablet actually caused my anxiety levels to increase further. It's a good indicator that all is not well if I struggle to limit myself and put the games down.

I sometimes think it's difficult to identify what is a hobby and what is self-care, activity or exercise. Attending a weekly yoga or Pilates session could fit neatly into any of those categories. Labels don't matter. What does matter is that, if the activity is enhancing your life and not causing ups and downs to your mood, then enjoy it and give gratitude for having it in your life.

I'm allowed to
take time for
myself

Just as it is!

Hormones and fluctuating moods

Most of the time, my bipolar is stable. The things that are embedded in my life such as routine, taking my medication, practising self-care and support from family and friends all play their part in keeping things ticking along without any issues. However, once a month, when I have my period and my hormones are running amok, I have a depressive spell. I always know it's coming. Its predictability means I can plan around it by having more rest and having a bit less in my diary and, even in the months when it's really bad, I am secure in the knowledge that it always passes in a few days.

This month, something different has happened. Instead of going back to that balanced mood afterwards, my mood has escalated to a level that falls into the early stages of hypomania. I haven't felt like this for a really long time and it's scary. Normally, when my mood starts to rise, I'm lucky in that my self-awareness kicks in and I'm able to put some extra strategies in place and relatively easily bring my mood back down. I rarely tell anyone it's happening. I simply assess what's happening in my life, where I'm doing too much and events that may have triggered the change. I get back into my routine and ensure that I'm getting enough sleep, eating well and exercising gently every day.

This time it's different, hard to explain really; my brain is flitting from thought to thought - it's too busy. If I think of something I need to do, I must do it immediately or it's lost in the void. This makes me a bit frantic. I'm listing a lot because my brain can't seem to hold information. I'm talking too much. My family have stopped listening to me, unable to pick out the important pieces of information I'm trying to share, so they just mute me in their heads. Then comes the frustration. Why aren't they listening to the important stuff? Why can't they pick it out? What makes this time different is that I've talked about where I'm at. I don't always tell people when my mood is rising, least of all my husband, because I need to protect him and there's no point worrying him unnecessarily as I can deal with this and get my mood down myself. I've been open with him this time and told him where my mood is right now. It means that I can ask for the support I need and other people are looking out for me and asking me where I'm at on the mood scale.

A question I've had to ask is "What has the trigger been for this?' It's important for me to see what I need to change and focus on not only for right now but also for the future so that I can try to avoid these triggers and prevent this from happening again. The triggers I've identified are lack of sleep; the stress of having my garden room built as the communication with the building team was poor and there were numerous delays; some extra hours at work; a lot to do in the house (why does a build in the garden affect so much in the house?); and not finding time for self-care. When I went wild swimming for the first time, I saw a sharp increase in mood afterwards (need to monitor this when I go wild swimming next week). Wow! That's quite a list!

Sleep feels like the biggest culprit but not necessarily the easiest to sort. We were up most of the night last Saturday as Fudge was sick. This was a big trigger. On Monday, I made a self-care decision to miss choir practice as I can't have my antipsychotic medication until 10 pm when I get in as opposed to 7 pm which is my normal time. I always struggle to get to sleep after choir practice so this felt like a positive step to get some extra sleep. So far so good. The antipsychotic medication is weird as sometimes it kicks in straight away and I'm sleepy, feeling a bit like I'm drunk, can't walk straight and slur my words. It's an awful feeling and, when it kicks in, sleep is imminent. However, sometimes, it doesn't kick in at all. It's so annoying as I've never worked out any pattern as to when it aids sleep and when I just feel awake. That's what's happened this week; despite my best efforts for a regular sleep pattern, I've not practised the best sleep routine that I could. I have the TV on in the bedroom when we go upstairs, especially as we often go up at 9 pm. Suddenly, before you know it, a few hours have passed and the TV is still on. Mornings are becoming tricky and it's difficult to get up. It's darker in the morning as it's mid-October now. And so, the problem continues.

I took a group of young people, who attend the theatre group I lead, to the theatre on Thursday night so I didn't get home until 11 pm; late meds again. It's just been a weird week. Today is Saturday and, to get to grips with this high mood, I need to focus on getting a good sleep routine and medication on time at 7 pm. I'm keeping a list of things I need to do but also asking for extra help from my husband and son, delegating as much as I can. Finding time for mindfulness practice, I still went to Pilates last night which felt like it helped. Tomorrow morning, I'll have a lie-in and a rest day. A key to getting back on track will be to maintain these changes for a few weeks at the bare minimum. I need to slow everything down, mind, daily schedule, more sleep and add more self-care and mindfulness practice as these have fallen by the wayside as life has become busier; and I need to keep talking about where I'm at as it makes me accountable. I can do this! I know I can because I've done it before but it will take focus and prioritising this over everything that hypomania makes me think is urgent and important but which, when I stop to think about it, isn't really.

Update: It's three weeks since I last wrote this "Just As It Is" piece but it feels much longer. My mood is still not stable. I'm using the Bipolar UK app to track where I'm at each day. This is really great because I can add words to describe how I feel and there's a notes section so I can add some detail if I want to. I've gone from an elevated mood with my mum telling me to talk slower on the phone, making quick decisions without thinking things through or over-thinking and making what feels like very sensible decisions. Aaarrrggghh! I'm in freefall. My mood has crashed back down. I'm crying a lot; my hormones have kicked in again and friends and family are pointing out things that seem perfectly reasonable to me but not to them so I'm confused and scared. Everything I'm putting into place to level me out is not very effective right now.

So, I decided to ask my psychiatrist to increase my antipsychotic medication to its previous dosage. I'm sure this will level me out, even if the side effects could be numbness, difficulty getting up in the morning and an inability to feel emotion. I need this! It's not a reflection of how hard I've tried to manage on my own; it's just an acceptance that I need something extra right now and hopefully, I can go back to my current dosage in a few months.

I have an appointment with my psychiatrist next week which isn't too long to wait. I know that, in bipolar terms, that could be a lifetime away so I called and spoke to one of the secretaries and explained what I needed. That was three days ago and I'm still waiting for a call back. I never need to call them but I know I'm just one of many to them, not the woman who never calls so it must be important. But I feel really positive about making the call. I'm taking control, not admitting defeat as I've tried everything in my mental health toolbox and medication increase is a strategy that I haven't needed to use for a long time - until now. This is all about the prevention of a mental health crisis; it is so much easier to intervene at this stage than wait until I'm past the stage of making these decisions for myself.

Update: Two weeks have passed since the dosage of my antipsychotic medication was increased. Life has become level and all seems well. It's a stark reminder of how challenging the side effects are combined with the knowledge that I've made the right decision and this is exactly what I need right now.

I'm numb, like my feelings and emotions have been turned down. I was watching Strictly Come Dancing the other night and I did not react to the performances as I wasn't sure what was good and what was mediocre. My husband says I'm distant and a neighbour commented the other day, "There's something not right about you today, are you ok?" Maintaining eye contact can be difficult and I'm withdrawing from social situations which is the opposite of how I usually am. I want to be at home and surrounded by my family. Mornings are more difficult as the medication is still in my system, a feeling similar to being hungover despite not having any alcohol for the past ten years. There's low-level paranoia that people are against me and lying although I've no proof. At work, I'm able to put on my happy face and, hopefully, I'm fooling everyone around me but who knows if that's the case. I'm having difficulty recalling the words I need, especially of items that I'm picturing in my head. I need to list all the time as my memory is shocking. If I don't do something in the moment, I can totally forget about it. However, despite all of this, I'm pleased with the result of the increased dosage. I'm much more stable and I can make rational decisions, informed choices and be in control. Well, most of the time! I am human after all and not just my diagnosis.

Update: It's about 6 months since I've gone back onto the higher dose of antipsychotics. I have no intention of asking for them to be reduced again. The side effects seemed to have levelled out and, whilst mornings are trickier, I've just altered my routine a little, reduced stress by being kind to myself and removed some unnecessary tasks. My mood is right where it should be and I'm living my life as I want to. It was definitely the right decision.

Final Thoughts

There was a time when I thought I would never be able to control my mood, I would never feel well again, and I didn't have much faith in my ability to learn all I needed. It definitely wasn't an easy journey to begin with but I believe my open-mindedness and ability to listen to the professionals and the advice given, along with my stubbornness and refusal to give in, has gotten me to where I am today.

What I describe as strategies and techniques in this book are skills. Like any new skill, you don't become proficient overnight. If you were learning an instrument, you would have lessons, be taught by a professional with years of experience and you would practise, practise, practise. Over time, it would become easier, you wouldn't have to focus as much on what you were doing and, in time, you would enjoy the experience. I always think of learning mental health methods in the same way and, if something is difficult to begin with, the reward when you succeed will undoubtedly be greater.

I think the most important things I've learned and the messages I want to share are, to be gentle with yourself and choose the language you use to talk to yourself with care, celebrate your successes no matter how small, and find what does and doesn't work for you. Find your tribe, those who "get you" and love you for your differences and uniqueness, those who don't judge you. Talk about what you are going through; the people who stick around choose to be there; they love you and genuinely want to help and support you. If you weren't putting a focus on your mental health and trying new things to help, you would probably feel worse than you do now even if everything currently feels awful. Progress is still progress, no matter how slowly you are going. If you are mentally unwell, this is separate from who you are as a person; the two things may seem intertwined but they really aren't. Use the tough times as opportunities to learn. Reflecting on what has happened will soon turn into reacting to what is happening as you can intervene in that moment rather than wait until afterwards to think things through.

I continue to practise and learn new things, to be curious about new experiences and ideas that may help me. Now that I'm well, I can enjoy life and, whilst my mood is stable, I'm always monitoring where I'm at in the background. My knowledge and self-awareness of my triggers and myself is excellent and this gives me the upper hand. I notice changes early and can step in and infiltrate a soaring or diminishing mood. This ability to react quickly is working really well and is helping me to prevent any episodes of note. I've got this! And you can too!

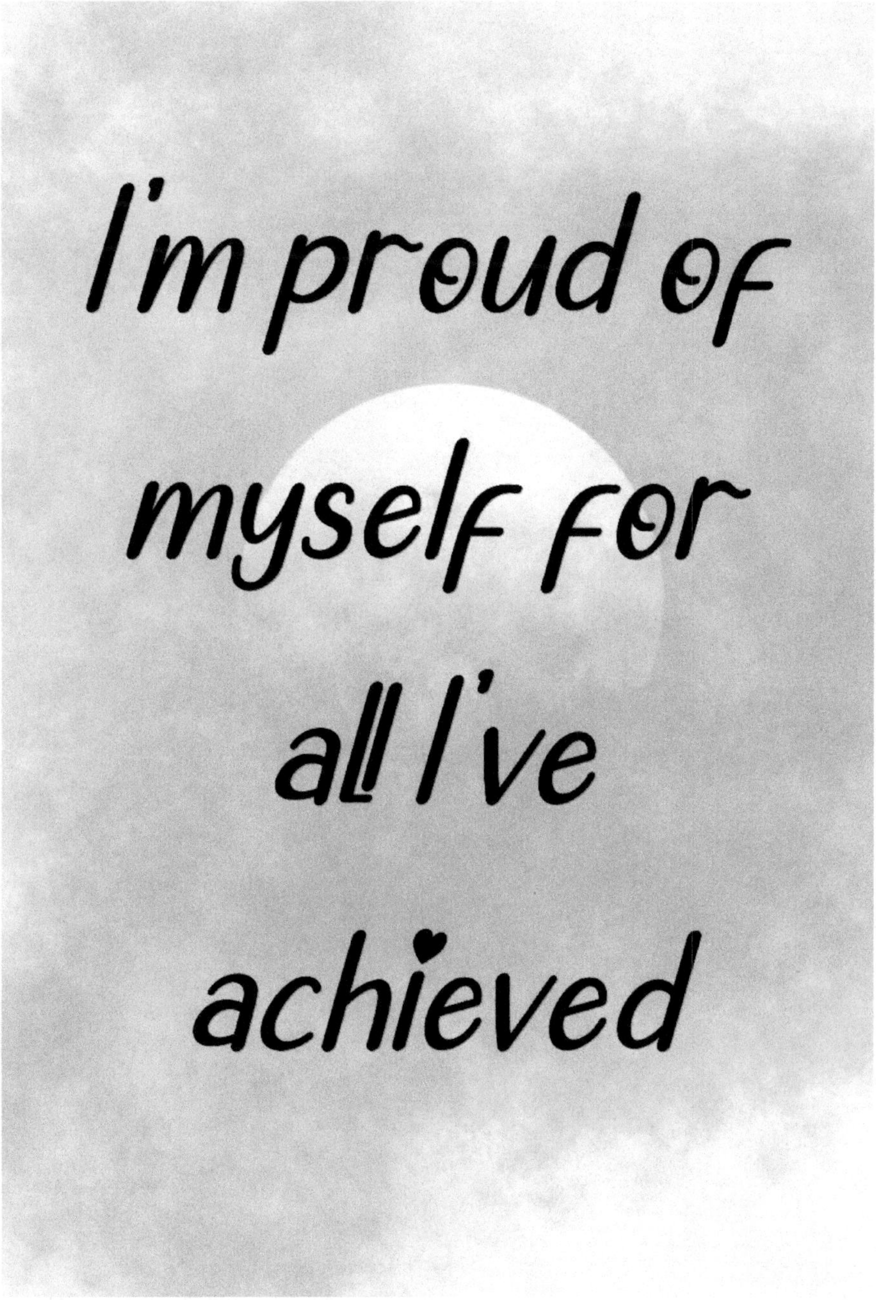
I'm proud of
myself for
all I've
achieved

Epilogue

29 January 2024

Yesterday, I finally got around to opening my Christmas presents. I just couldn't face it before. I've written this book as my true authentic self so I wanted to share what's happened over Christmas and the New Year.

On 23 December 2023, I was admitted as an informal patient to a secure psychiatric ward in the midst of a manic episode. Being informal means that you go into the hospital voluntarily as opposed to being sectioned, which is when you are detained under the Mental Health Act and have no choice but to be admitted. I always say that being informal is like the line in the song "Hotel California" by the Eagles *"You can check in any time you like but you can never leave."* There are still a lot of restrictions on what you can and can't do.

I honestly thought I would never need another hospital admission (my last was over 10 years ago), that I was stable and so knowledgeable about my triggers and early warning signs that I was winning the fight against bipolar. I knew my mood was rising in the months before. I was using lots of strategies and, whilst my mood did come back down, it wasn't staying there and kept bobbing back up.

It's easy to reflect after a bipolar episode as to whether it was a manic or depressive episode and to analyse what you ought to have done. The difference for me this time is that it genuinely is a setback and not a relapse. I can't unlearn all the knowledge I now have about myself, the strategies I've collected over the years or the wisdom I have gained.

As an inpatient on a secure ward, you become institutionalised pretty quickly but I was able to use my time wisely. I spent time with others and embraced the offerings from the occupational therapists, at art classes and using the gym. I meditated every day and gave myself Reiki. I read and did puzzles (word searches on my own and jigsaws with others). I spoke honestly with the staff about how I was feeling and, on my last day, I was able to sing with the music therapist. Thankfully, this made the four weeks I was in the hospital go pretty quickly, as I was miles away from home and, as there were no beds locally, my visitors were few and far between.

Now I'm home and I've time to reflect on what caused the episode in the first place; a reduction of my lithium as it had got too high in my bloodstream; late nights and disruption to my antipsychotic medication; taking on extra work commitments; over-confidence in how much I could do and how well I could push the limits of my bipolar whilst keeping it stable; and not asking for help when I needed it.

I'm reassessing what's important in my life and what's surplus to requirements. Some things are dropping out of my routine so I'm not overdoing it but, as things are removed, space is created for those things that should have been given higher priority, many of which are written about in this book. However, I'm human and constantly learning, growing and creating.

I'm doing the best I can at any given moment and that is enough.

LAURA'S LIFE LESSONS

YOU ALWAYS HAVE A CHOICE.

PEOPLE WANT TO HELP, SO ASK FOR HELP WHEN YOU NEED IT AND ACCEPT THEIR OFFERS.

BE OPEN MINDED TO TRYING NEW THINGS, SOME WILL WORK FOR YOU AND AND SOME WON'T BUT YOU WON'T KNOW IF YOU DON'T TRY.

KNOWING WHAT ISN'T HELPFUL TO YOU IS JUST AS VALUABLE AS THE KNOWLEDGE OF WHAT DOES.

LEARNING A NEW SKILL TAKES PRACTICE, PATIENCE AND PERSEVERANCE. THESE NEW SKILLS PROBABLY WON'T HELP STRAIGHT AWAY BUT DON'T GIVE UP TOO EASILY, GIVE IT TIME.

A SLIP UP, IS A SLIP UP NOT A RELAPSE. YOU CAN'T UNLEARN YOUR NEW STRATEGIES AND TECHNIQUES. USE THIS AS ANOTHER LEARNING OPPORTUNITY, DRAW A LINE AND START AGAIN.

YOU HAVE THE POWER IN YOU TO ALTER YOUR THOUGHT PATTERNS AND ALTER THE PATH OF YOUR LIFE.

MENTAL AND PHYSICAL HEALTH IS INTRINSICALLY LINKED.
THE JOURNEY TOWARDS BETTER MENTAL AND PHYSICAL HEALTH IS ONGOING AND THE PATH WILL NOT FOLLOW A STRAIGHT LINE.

IT REALLY IS OK NOT TO BE OK. THIS FEELING IS TEMPORARY AND WILL BE REPLACED BY ANOTHER FEELING WHICH IS ALSO TEMPORARY.

Resources

Bipolar UK
www.bipolaruk.org

Mind
www.mind.org.uk

Samaritans
www.samaritains.org

Shout
Mental health text support
www.giveusashout.org
Text SHOUT to 85258

Pumpkin and Friends Charity
www.pumpkinandfriendscharity.com

Autumn Blossoms
Emily Webster
www.autumnblossoms.co.uk

Lynette Allen
www.awomansblessing.com

Julie Keen
www.julieunbound.co.uk

WEA
Adult learning courses – free to those on certain benefits
www.wea.org.uk

Andrea Jackson
www.radiantwoman.me

Addiction Resources

Addiction support – www.nhs.uk

www.turning-point.co.uk

www.smartrecovery.org.uk

www.actiononaddiction.org.uk

Laura's Recommended podcasts

Bipolar UK
Let's Talk Bipolar – Emma Belle

Extraordinary People – Katie Piper

Happy Place – Fearne Cotton

Mad World – Bryony Gordon

Open Mind – Frankie Bridge

Radio 4 Woman's Hour

Acknowledgements

Firstly, I want to thank the amazing team at Russell-Alexander Publishing for believing that people would want to hear my story, for guiding me and gently nurturing my writing whilst providing the individualised support I needed to ensure my mental health remained stable and was unaffected by any stress or over-excitement.

To my English teachers at school and college, Miss Walsh and Mr. Limbert. Miss Walsh always said she took two evenings to mark our class's work, one evening for my short story and the other evening to mark everyone else's. I thought 24 pages of writing was short! They both instilled a love of writing in me and the self-confidence in my ability, without which this book may have remained unwritten.

To my friend, Catherine Parry, not only for her gorgeous artwork but also for her belief in this project and her support. I always felt my direction was clearer after a cuppa and a chat. Her questions got me thinking and ultimately got me to write a better book.

To my friend, Amy Kelly, for her photography skills. She doesn't call it a Goddess photoshoot for nothing; you truly do feel like a goddess.

To Andrea Jackson, Julie Keen, Nikki Hollins, Lynette Allen, Stevie Foster, Emily Webster and Chris Summers who opened my eyes to a whole new world and way of living; who have expertly guided me and taught me life-changing skills that have not only empowered me but ensured I have an overflowing toolbox of mental health strategies to dip into whenever I need to; thus enabling me to manage my mental health. I will be eternally grateful to you all.

About the Author

Laura Bartlam BSc Hons, PGCE, PGDip

Laura's lifelong, complicated physical and mental health issues have led her on a journey of self-discovery. She's found techniques and strategies that allow her to manage the fine balance of these conditions.

In her writing, she shares her experiences of what she's learned so far to empower others in their journeys. Explaining why she has spoken so openly about her own physical and mental health challenges, she said "I'm using my darkest days to help others out of theirs."

Laura was born in Scotland but currently lives in West Yorkshire with her husband, her son and her two dogs. She is a mental health advocate, Reiki Master and learning disability specialist.

Printed in Great Britain
by Amazon

42058595R00116